ROADS AND TRACKWAYS OF
THE LAKE DISTRICT

Roads and Trackways of
The
Lake District

Brian Paul Hindle

British Library Cataloguing in Publication
Data

Hindle, Paul
    Roads and Trackways of The Lake
    District
    1. Roads — England — Lake District
    — History
    I. Title
    388.1'09427'   HE363.G74L34

To my parents

ISBN 0 86190 121 5

Printed in the UK by Billings of Worcester
for the publishers Moorland Publishing
Co Ltd, 9-11 Station Street, Ashbourne,
Derbyshire, DE6 1DE England.
Telephone: (0335) 44486

Contents

Introduction

The Lake District is arguably the most written-about part of the British Isles, and one might have thought that, by now, there was little more to be said about it. There is a plethora of books covering virtually every aspect of the history and topography of the region, dealing with specific topics (ranging from abbeys to mines) as well as with specific local areas. And yet, apart from the present author's earlier booklet, no-one has attempted a history of Lakeland's roads and trackways.

One has only to glance through the indexes of any of the standard 'Lake District' texts to see how roads are neglected. Roads are taken for granted not only in these local studies but also in virtually every historical study of Britain; various authors have written much about travellers, and about the growth of trade in particular, but have hardly given a thought to how people travelled from one place to the next. No-one has asked why certain lines of travel have been preferred at various times, while others, once busy thoroughfares, have virtually disappeared. The number of studies that has been produced of roads in specific areas of Britain is very small but it does include two companion volumes to this one, dealing with the Peak District and Wales respectively. The study of the growth of our road system is fundamental to the understanding of all the other socio-economic features of the landscape. Roads are vital to man, and their history is inextricably tied in with the growth (or decline) of population, towns, industry, agriculture, and of course, trade. Thus roads cannot be considered in isolation; their development has to be related to the rest of the landscape, otherwise their study would be nothing more than a drab list of construction dates and tedious descriptions of the routes involved. The social, economic and political influences on man and the landscape determine how many roads there are, and how important those roads are in relation to eath other, but it is the physical landscape which determines the precise routes which they take.

The approach adopted here is a chronological one — starting with Roman roads and working through to the turnpikes and enclosure roads. It is, however, difficult to maintain a strict chronological approach throughout, for the evidence for different types of roads starts to become much greater after the Middle Ages, and it is better to look at drove roads, say, in a single section rather than spreading out the references to them (which are dated between the twelfth and nineteenth centuries) over several chapters. There are very few roads which can be described simply as, say, medieval, for most of those in use at that time were created long before, and are still in use today. This highlights one of the problems about studying roads, namely that they rarely tend to be of just one period; for instance a road may have been built by the Romans and used ever since. Another pitfall in studying roads is to look at a succession of individual routes as if they were isolated from all the other roads round about; roads must be studied as a system or network, and one which changes in time. Only for the Roman and turnpike roads is it possible and useful to look at individual routes simply because they were planned and made individually.

The geographical area covered by this book is rather wider than its title might suggest, for it would be rather pointless just to look at the roads inside 'Lakeland' in isolation from the surrounding area. If we take the rather arbitrary boundary of the National Park as delimiting Lakeland, then this would exclude most of the Roman roads, while the Shap road runs along its border for many miles; Kendal, which was such an important centre for trade and travel in the eighteenth century, would be omitted, as would any consideration of travel in Low Furness and the route across the sands. Accordingly, the book considers virtually all of the new county of Cumbria, but stops at the Solway and Roman Wall in the north, and at the Pennine ridge of Cross Fell in the north-east. The book does concentrate on the roads of the Lake District, but does not ignore those of the surrounding area.

Although numerous maps are provided to illustrate the text, it is only through looking at large scale Ordnance Survey maps that the full picture can be obtained, whether you are in the comfort of your armchair, or actually out in the field. The one-inch tourist map of the Lake District, plus the one-inch or new 1:50,000 maps of the surrounding area are basic requirements, while for detailed study, 1:25,000 (2½in) or 1:10,000 (6in) maps may be required. Grid references are given throughout the book to places not immediately obvious, and the OS maps are necessary to locate them. The prefix letters have been omitted, but they are needed if you wish to buy a larger scale map.[1]

The aims of this book are twofold — first to tell the story of a particular aspect of Lakeland's history and landscape, and second to encourage more local research. Research is not an elitist occupation undertaken by pedagogues in ivory towers — certainly Salford University where this is being written could never be described as an ivory tower. Anyone who has an interest in roads, local knowledge of an area, and above all imagination, can help to 'expand the sum of human knowledge'. A car and a pair of hiking boots are also a great help! The present author's interest grew from the combination of a love of fell-walking and an academic interest in old maps and medieval England. It will soon become obvious that there are large gaps in our knowledge of Lakeland roads, which can only be remedied by local research, perhaps dealing with only one or two parishes. Such work will start to give a much more detailed picture of the development of the road system than can be attempted at present. To this end, references are given throughout the book, both to aid the general reader who wants to know more on a certain topic, and to give some idea of the wide range of source materials to those who may wish to do some detailed local research. In addition, the local record offices and local history libraries at Carlisle, Kendal, Barrow and Preston are repositories of vast amounts of unworked material. At the very least the archivists will be glad to see someone who has not come in simply to trace their family roots!

After the initial research in the library and archives comes the rather more energetic part of research — actually getting out into the countryside to follow old routes, whether on foot or by car, in order to see for example why the Romans or the turnpike surveyors chose a particular route, why a packhorse route or drove road went a particular way, or why another route has shifted its course over the years. What may be unclear from the map or the historical record may be stunningly clear on the ground.

There is little or no evidence for any roads in Cumbria before the Romans arrived; there were only a few people living in the area then, and any tracks which they created have not survived, or have not had any apparent effect on later roads. Prehistoric man certainly inhabited parts of Cumbria, but virtually all he has left behind are odd groups of cairns and stone circles. The only slight clue to a prehistoric route is connected with the 'axe factories' known to have existed in and around Langdale — the rough axes were probably taken to the coast for polishing, and then on by sea to the rest of Britain. It would be fatuous to draw a line on a map and call it an 'axe route', though no doubt someone either has or will eventually do just that. Devotees of Alfred Watkins and his 'ley lines' will be disappointed to find no consideration of his theories here, for any objective study of his curious ideas reveals only random alignments and associations, and his notions of a race of stone-age road builders are best forgotten. Instead, we must turn straightaway to consider the achievements of the first Lakeland road builders — namely the Romans.

Roman
Roads

2.1 The Roman Invasion

The history of the Roman occupation of Cumbria is complicated, and many of the details are often unclear, but an outline of the story will help in the understanding of how the road network grew. The Roman road system in Cumbria was not designed and built as a complete network, but grew in response to changing military needs, often reflecting events north of the border. Lines of penetration came first, these were essentially supply lines for the armies, linking the earliest temporary camps; the establishment of more permanent forts and more roads to administer and supply the whole area came later. Eventually routes with no further military value were abandoned. Thus it was not an uncommon practice for the Romans to build their roads first, and the forts later; this explains the unusual sites of some forts, and their even spacing along some main roads. It should also be remembered that the forts were built at different dates, and many went out of use for long periods when not required; Fig 2.1 is an attempt to show how the forts came in and out of use in the first hundred years of Roman rule in Cumbria. This is fundamental to understanding how the road system grew, and often it enables additions to the network to be dated.

The Romans had been in Britain for 45 years before they attempted the conquest of the Brigantes, the tribe occupying most of the north-west England.[1] Under Agricola in AD78 or 79 they seem to have marched up both sides of the Pennines from their legionary fortresses at Chester and York, building the first roads and forts in the area as they went, and continuing to the very edge of the Highlands of Scotland. Thus the conquest of Cumbria was only a small part of a much greater plan. By AD84 they had built the forts along the main road to the north, and along the Stainmore road and the Stanegate, adding the roads to Kirkbride, Papcastle and Maryport soon after. Watercrook and Ambleside forts were also probably built during this period (Fig 2.2). However, by AD87 the Romans had retreated to the Clyde-Forth line, and in 105 back to the Stanegate itself.

In about 120 came the decision to build Hadrian's Wall along this new frontier, together with a Military Way immediately behind it. The Wall was continued by a series of milefortlets and stone towers along the coast beyond Bowness as if the planners intended the fortifications and the accompanying road to continue at least as far as Maryport. The building of the Wall set a definite northern limit to the Roman province of Britannia, and imperial policy was clearly designed to defend the area in order to develop and exploit its resources.

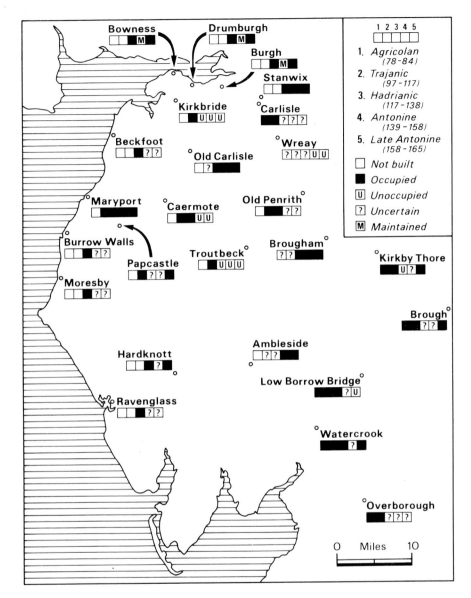

Fig 2.1   Roman Forts in Cumbria

Most of the remaining forts in Cumbria date from this period; the area was fully occupied for the first time, with between thirteen and twenty-one forts in use. The next change in policy came with the death of Hadrian in 138; the following year saw the reconquest of southern Scotland and the building of the Antonine Wall as the new northern frontier of the Province. Hadrian's Wall was abandoned as a defensive line, although it and the forts along it were maintained. During this period many of the other Cumbrian forts seem to have been unoccupied, with probably only Stanwix, Papcastle, Maryport, Hardknott and Ambleside (and possibly Ravenglass, Old Penrith and Brougham) still retaining troops.

Serious unrest broke out in 155, and the Antonine Wall was under threat until it was finally abandoned in 163. This coincided with a general re-fortification of

11

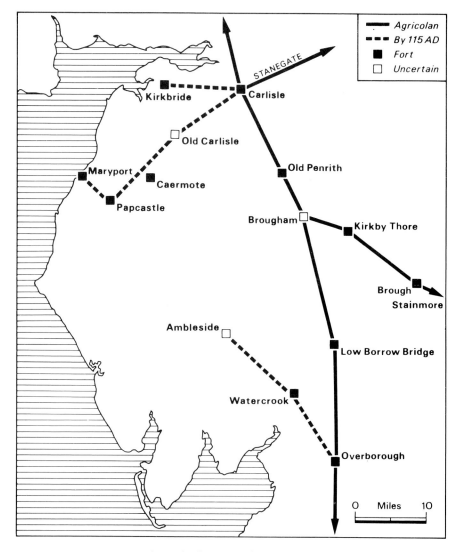

Fig 2.2   Roman Forts and Roads about AD84

northern England, and especially of Cumbria; between seventeen and twenty-four forts were now occupied and the original turf of the western section of Hadrian's Wall was rebuilt in stone. After this, more settled times prevailed and the number of forts occupied at any one time decreased, although the Wall forts always remained garrisoned. The road system was by then probably fully established, and would no doubt also have begun to fulfil the needs of the growing civil population of the area, notably in Carlisle whose early fort had given way to a town which in due course had become a prosperous city. The Roman army remained in Cumbria for just over three hundred years, its effective withdrawal beginning in 383. The Romans left their mark on the landscape not only in the most obvious feature of the Wall, but also in their system of forts and settlements, many of which have become towns today. Their road system was a comprehensive one, and most of this too is still in use; the present state of knowledge of the system is as shown in Fig 2.3. Each route will be described later in the chapter.

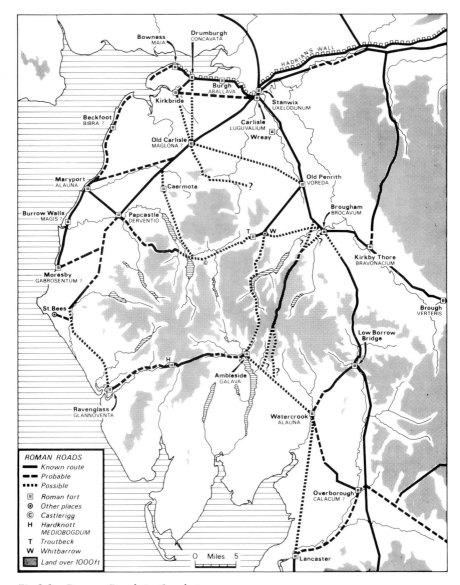

Fig 2.3   Roman Roads in Cumbria

Throughout this chapter modern place-names will be used; the correct Roman names for many places are still uncertain.[2] The most recent interpretation is shown in Fig 2.3.

2.2   Roman Roads

Roman roads vary a good deal in their constructional details; typically they consist of an *agger* (the raised central portion) of various widths, often bounded by ditches on each side. Excavation has revealed that local materials were normally used in their construction, varying from beach pebbles to quarried rock. Roads vary along their length quite considerably; their widths are not consistent, they are embanked in some places and not in others, and they may or may not be metalled. It certainly seems that great latitude was given to the engineers who built each short section. The net result is that whether or not their course has since been ploughed over, they may or may not be visible today.

It always used to be said that Roman roads were *straight*, and this simple over-statement was perhaps summed up most memorably in *1066 And All That*, where the authors stated unequivocally that 'the Roman roads ran absolutely straight in all directions and all led to Rome.'[3] A rather better description, however, is that they were *direct*; often a road may be seen leading directly towards its destination while still many miles away only to change direction in order to gain some advantage, usualy to avoid the wet ground of valley bottoms. We shall see this happening very clearly at the northern end of High Street. Steep gradients on the other hand were rarely avoided and this reflects the primary purpose of Roman roads which was the rapid movement of men and pack animals; carts and wagons would have required physical assistance on some steep sections. The standard method of laying out long straight alignments had to be modified or even abandoned in many hilly areas, but even here the roads still proceed in a series of short straight lengths rather than curves; indeed earlier trackways may have been followed and improved to Roman standards. In such areas the roads also tend to be narrower especially when they are terraced across a hillside, or where they go through cuttings. Equally the narrowness may have been due to a shortage of material, or that such a road was never developed beyond the pioneer stage.

Archaeological evidence for Roman roads had traditionally been very important; F. Haverfield made this absolutely clear in a comment on a paper about a possible Roman road in Eskdale: 'any exploration of a Roman road must be called cursory which omits the spade . . . . Certainly the first thing to be done here is to dig.'[4] More recently, trends in archaeology have gone to the opposite extreme, so that some archaeologists now regard digging as the last resort; no doubt a balance between these two extreme views will be achieved in practice. Fortunately sectioning a road does little harm, as only a few feet in many miles may need to be excavated in order to establish whether or not it is Roman. It is, of course, difficult to section a road which is still in use, and covered with tarmac!

The types of evidence which must be used in order to postulate a Roman road are many and varied. Something may be gleaned from the examination of the sole surviving contemporary written source, namely the *Antonine Itinerary*, which lists many of the main roads of the empire. The *Itinerary* is a collection of 225 routes throughout the Roman Empire, fifteen of which are in Britain. It is impossible to date the *Itinerary* as it evidently underwent a long process of compilation; some routes could relate to the early second century, while the final form was not reached until about AD300. Three of the British routes enter Cumbria, two cover the route from Carlisle to York, while the third is from Ravenglass to Whitchurch.

The larger scale maps and plans of the Ordnance Survey are vital for research. The one-inch tourist map of the Lake District and the newer 1:50,000 scale maps are excellent for looking at the overall alignments of Roman roads, but for detailed work the 2½in and 6in to one mile maps (1:25,000 and 1:10,560/1:10,000) are vital, for they show field boundaries, and many more place-names. Older editions of these maps are better for our purposes than newer ones, for they may show hedges and walls which have been removed, and place-names which have gone out of use. Any old map of an area may well be worth consulting, whether it be an early estate plan, or one of the one-inch maps drawn in the late eighteenth century such as Jeffery's map of Westmorland (1770) or Donald's Cumberland (1774) (see chapter 4).

As will become very obvious during this chapter, many Roman roads have yet to be fully traced on the ground, and there is great scope for the amateur Roman road hunter. The first step is to read all that has been written previously about a particular route — for features may have been observed by earlier antiquarians or achaeologists which have since been destroyed, whether by enclosure, ploughing or simple erosion.[6] Second, old documents may refer to Roman roads, and may give place-names that are no longer used. Third, photographs, especially aerial ones taken at oblique angles, can be of great use, for many features can often be seen only from the air, perhaps as soil or crop marks, or as shadows when the sun is low.

Place-names have been widely used to trace old roads; the list is long but includes *Street* (*Streat, Stretton, Stratford*, etc), *Gate* (meaning a road), *Stone* or *Stane* (referring to the stony nature of the road), *Old Street, High Street* (when found in open country, and also rendered locally as Hugill, from the Norse *ha-geil*), *Street Field, Causey* or *Causeway* and even *Borrans* (an Old English word referring to a pile of stones) and *Cold Harbour* (this last name implies somewhere to shelter from the cold, and curiously often indicates a nearby Roman road). Parish boundaries are another useful guide, more especially in lowland areas which were settled quite early in the Dark Ages. The simple reason for this is that when the Anglo-Saxons and Danes started to settle in England and to begin to build up the network of villages, they deliberately chose sites away from the Roman roads, knowing that any marauding armies would use those roads and hopefully leave the villages in peace. Thus their villages were sited a mile or two away from Roman roads, and those roads often became the boundaries between the villages. The prime example of this in Britain is Watling Street (the present-day A5); it has virtually no early settlements on it, and is a parish boundary for most of its length. Certainly Roman roads with their prominent *aggers* must have made excellent boundaries.

Roman roads tend to connect known Roman sites (bearing in mind that in the early days the roads were sometimes built first), and another useful clue is to look for good crossing places of rivers (also bearing in mind that a river may have shifted its course in the last 2,000 years). If a short alignment is known, then a preliminary step is to extend that line in both directions in the search for further evidence.

All this work is a vital first step in tracing the course of any supposed Roman road, before venturing into the field. Nevertheless, it is the examination in the field which is the most exciting part of the process, for the options open to the Roman surveyor will start to become much more obvious, and minor features which cannot be shown on a map can be observed at first hand. Nevertheless it has to be realised that obtaining absolute proof that a track across open country is Roman is very difficult; in only a few cases is it possible to follow a track directly from the gate of one Roman fort to the gate of another. Ultimately, of course, the excavation of a section of road may be required, and this should be entrusted to a trained archaeologist, and then fully recorded and published. Permission to cross private land should always be sought, happily most of the Lake District has virtually no access restrictions, but the farmland around the fringes of the hills does not come into this category.

The rest of this chapter will look in detail at the four Roman roads which run through the core of the Lake District, and then deal with the roads of the surrounding area, starting with the south-eastern approaches, and working anti-clockwise from Lancaster via Brougham and Carlisle around to Ravenglass.

2.3 High Street
Of all the Roman roads in the Lake District, High Street is certainly the best known, for its route along the high fells of eastern Lakeland has given the highest of those hills its name, and its course can be followed for many miles by the adventurous

walker.[7] The road was referred to in a thirteenth century charter as 'Brethstrett'[8] (ie the paved way of the Britons) and its route along the ridge at a height of over 2,000ft for eight miles was the sort of ridgeway preferred in pre-Roman times, largely because it was above the tree line, making progress much easier. There is, however, absolutely no evidence of this route being in use before the Romans came. If the central section of this road is obvious, its route at each end is not at all clear, and has been the subject of much debate. Thus, in this case it is easiest to adopt the unusual procedure of starting from the summit and working towards each end in turn.

The summit of High Street (441110) which stands 2,718ft above sea level, has an easy-going grassy top, a route well known and well used by all manner of people from Roman soldiers right through to present-day hikers, not to mention its use as a racecourse.[9] Near the summit, the road does not take the crest of the hill, but lies a hundred yards or so to the west; and has been breached in two places by erosion. There are numerous other tracks made later by packhorses and of course by modern fell-walkers.

North The route northwards leads down into the Straits of Riggindale and then, after climbing to High Raise (458134) it maintains virtually a straight line northwards for 3½ miles along the ridge to Loadpot Hill; the road and the parish boundary coinciding for most of the way (Fig 2.4a). Approaching Loadpot Hill, the road leaves this alignment to curve around the west side of the summit, and then at 461198, it turns north-eastwards on a new alignment which, if followed directly, would take it straight to the fort at Brougham, still some 7½ miles distant. The road can be traced by the short green sward covering it which contrasts with the heather of the rest of the fell. It has been sectioned at several places; near Loadpot Hill the section revealed a top layer of gravel, 9in thick at the centre, but thinning towards the sides, then an 8in thick layer of peat, and finally a 2ft thick base of larger, rougher but evidently quarried stones, probably from the nearby quarry of Loadpot Hole (459185). A little further north on the descent to Elder Beck the road had

High Street, the summit

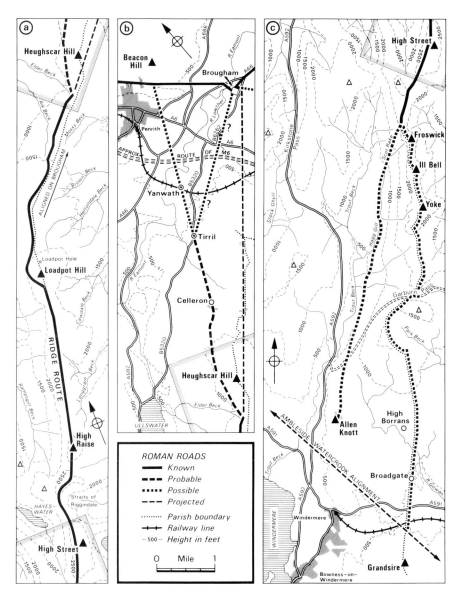

Fig 2.4   High Street

curbstones, 9in square and 10 or 11ft apart, though it is doubtful that the road was metalled throughout its whole length.[10]

The road continues on this new alignment as far as the crossing of Elder Beck (482222) where it has again been studied in some detail, revealing an older crossing place a short distance downstream from the present ford.[11] But it is at this point that real difficulties begin. Traditionally, the road has been assumed to have gone around the west side of Heughscar Hill to Celleron and thence to Tirril, presumably heading for a crossing of the River Eamont near Yanwath, in order to join the main road to Carlisle beneath Beacon Hill (Fig 2.4b).

Almost from the start this route is difficult to follow; its curious curving route around Heughscar disappears from the ground just beyond the Scar (486238), and although Ordnance Survey maps have long shown this route continuing as far as Tirril, its course is now impossible to trace.[12] Beyond Tirril the evidence for its course is poor, and it is not at all clear why the road, which had previously been heading straight for Brougham, should suddenly start to make for a different destination. In fact, Thomas Hay, writing about the alignments near Elder Beck, noted another road going north-east from that point, over the summit of Heughscar Hill, through what he calls 'much better country'.[13]

This change in the landscape is principally geological, for the route now runs over limestone, and the short ascent of the hill is marked by a series of parallel ruts which could well be Roman. Unfortunately, much of the top of the hill is covered with what look like World War II tank tracks! Overall, though, this is a more logical route for the road to have taken, but it still awaits verification in the field; the one piece of supporting map evidence is that it is aligned with a parish boundary (albeit not an absolutely straight one) for the first three miles (as far as 514259). It would be useful to have more field evidence for either route, especially for their respective crossings of the Eamont and Lowther. It is of course possible that *both* are Roman routes, built at different times in response to different circumstances, or that only the Yanwath road was built, but with a branch to Brougham from Tirril.

South Returning now to the summit, the route southwards skirts Thornthwaite Crag, and is shown by the Ordnance Survey as descending steeply into Hagg Gill *via* a route known as Scot Rake (Fig 2.4c). This well marked groove in the hillside is probably best seen from the Kirkstone Pass road when there is a light covering of snow or when the sun is just getting high enough to bring the Rake into relief. R.G. Collingwood described its route continuing for four miles as far south as Allen Knott, once thought to have been a Roman fort.[14] Indeed there is still a track along most of this route, though it shows little real indication of being Roman in origin. It is rarely straight, and the terrain and vegetation would have made it a difficult route in Roman times. It is quite likely that Collingwood had simply assumed that the road descended Scot Rake, and that he then set out to look for its continuation. In the early nineteenth century, Scot Rake was used by peat carriers taking peat down

High Street, the final clear length of agger *going north(475215)*

18

to Windermere in the days before the arrival of the railway provided cheaper supplies of coal; it is therefore entirely possible that Scot Rake is not Roman in origin at all. It seems unlikely that the Romans, having built a road along the relatively easy treeless ridge, should leave it so soon, although there is the consideration of the lack of a water supply for horses on the ridge. What is more important, however, is to consider the road's destination. Some early researchers suggested that it must have been heading for the fort at Ambleside but any direct connection is not far short of a physical impossibility, and no link has ever been found.

Let us suppose, for the moment, that the road did not leave the ridge at Scot Rake, but continued along the ridge, skirting the summits of Froswick and Ill Bell, before descending to Yoke and what is now the Garburn Pass. A Corn Rent map of 1838 marks two short lengths of track on Yoke at 436062 which are marked as 'Roman Road'; this indicates at least that the track had been constructed, and was then regarded as ancient. Having left the ridge and followed the higher ground around the headwaters of Park Beck, the Roman engineers might have reverted to their normal practice of laying out a straight alignment. From 433029 a parish boundary still runs directly, with only one slight change of direction, for 3½ miles to the small hill of Grandsire (432973), which is itself very close to a line drawn directly between the forts at Ambleside and Watercrook. The view of the line of this parish boundary from Grandsire is very impressive. Moreover there are farms called Broadgate and High Borrans on or near this route, although one cannot take such evidence as conclusive. The discovery of a fort near the Grandsire 'junction' would be most interesting, and verification of this southern part of the High Street route is needed virtually throughout its whole length, as is that of the Watercrook-Ambleside route, to which we must next turn our attention.

2.4 Watercrook to Ravenglass
This route has as many difficulties of interpretaton as High Street, but for very different reasons; on the one hand we know that it was an important route from

High Street, the wall following the parish boundary coming directly towards the hill of Grandsire

contemporary written evidence, but on the other hand most of its length has yet to be traced on the ground. It is listed in the *Antonine Itinerary* as part of the route from Ravenglass to Whitchurch; its first four stages are as follows:

Iter X	Itinerary Roman Miles	Actual Statute Miles	
Clanoventa			Ravenglass
	18	20	
Galava			Ambleside
	12	13	
Alone			Watercrook
	19	13	
Galacum			Overborough
	27	30	
Bremetonnaci			Ribchester

Although there are discrepancies in the mileages which may be due to original inaccuracy or to poor copying of manuscripts, the correspondence is quite good overall. It should be borne in mind, however that the Roman mile in use in Britain

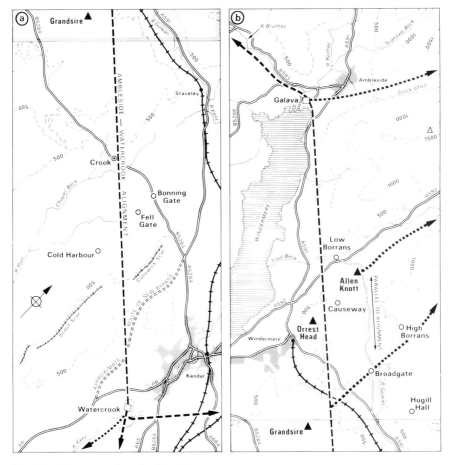

Fig 2.5   Watercrook to Ambleside

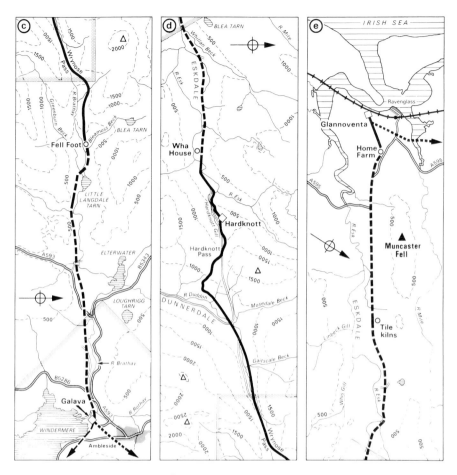

Fig 2.6   Ambleside to Ravenglass

varied somewhat, and was between four and eight percent *shorter* than the statute mile; on the Solway coast, for example, the average distance between the milefortlets is 1,620yd.

It has been claimed that the *Itinerary* lists the main post roads of the Roman Empire, and even if this is not strictly true, this route was still important enough to be listed in detail far away in Rome. And yet only 6 of the 33 miles from Watercrook to Ravenglass can be seen on the ground or on the map in any form at all. Of the section from Watercrook to Ambleside, virtually nothing is known, nor has much attention been given to its route. A straight line joining the two forts passes over much rough country, and it is always possible that the route took an easier but less direct course up the Kent Valley as far as Staveley, and then across to Windermere and Ambleside — effectively the same route which the A591 takes today (Fig 2.5). Scanning the map reveals several road place-names and even a *Cold Harbour* (479931). a name always suggestive of a nearby Roman road. Of course, the question of the route taken by the southern end of High Street, namely whether it led to Allen Knott or to Grandsire, is inextricably linked with any discussion of our present route. Proving the course of any one of these routes should help to settle the whole question. For the moment we are left with several possibilities, but no clear answers.

From Ambleside, the road must have taken a course along the south side of the

Wrynose Bottom, the Roman road can be seen crossing Gaitscale Gill

River Brathay but it does not first appear on the ground until it has climbed into Little Langdale (Fig 2.6). In 1920 at a site a few yards east of the footbridge and ford connecting Little Langdale and Tilberthwaite, R.G. Collingwood observed a section of road, some 60ft long by 10ft wide with large foundation and kerb stones (317029). Unfortunately, the rest of his description of the route in this article is highly fanciful.[15] The continuation is unknown — it may have remained south of the river and of Little Langdale Tarn, or may have crossed the river without much ado; in either case it would have had to avoid the marshy ground above the tarn. It has next been spotted in the field to the north of Fell Foot Farm, right at the start of Wrynose Pass and continuing the line of the present road eastwards instead of turning south through the farm as the modern road does (299033).[16]

Once on Wrynose Pass we are on safer ground, and the road from here has been the subject of a classic description by Ian Richmond based on field work done in 1946.[17] Indeed, this central section of the road is well preserved, and has almost continuous remains until Eskdale is reached, reflecting the lack of intensive agriculture which has removed so much of the evidence in the better farmed lowlands. The Roman road first appears as a shelf in the hillside just before the crossing of Wrynose Beck, soon regaining its apparent original width of some 18ft (285033). It lies some 75yd above the present road at the crossing, and continues along a rather better line. The two routes meet just before the Three Shires Stone, and then for about 80yd they both use the same route at the very summit of the pass. For the descent, the Roman road once again keeps above the present road, along a terraced shelf, and the two roads cross again at about 266023. Precisely where the Roman road crossed the stream is not clear, but its course soon becomes plain on the north side of the Duddon where it runs in a straight line for almost a mile as a causeway 24ft wide, perhaps best seen just beyond Gaitscale Gill (258021), and clearly marked as a footpath on the 1:25,000 map. The road probably crossed the Duddon again at 252019 where there is a good shallow fording point and it then follows the modern road until crossing the river for the final time just before Cockley Beck Bridge.

It is in the ascent of Hard Knott Pass that the Roman and present-day roads are farthest apart; the Romans chose an entirely different route which continued down the valley for another three-quarters of a mile, the relict causeway here being some 20ft wide. Beyond Black Hall the road starts to climb the pass by a series of zigzags, again clearly shown on the 1:25,000 map, which takes it to the top of the pass. It rejoins the modern road just beyond the latter's summit and remains on or close to it until the modern road takes its infamous steep left-hand bend; here the Roman

Hard Knott Pass. The Roman road formerly went straight on where the modern road has a very steep and tight bend. The Roman parade ground near the fort can be seen in the middle distance

road goes straight on, remaining above the present road until it swings into the southeast gate of Hardknott fort.[18] Roman soldiers no doubt greeted their arrival at the fort and its bath house with great relief after the arduous ten miles from Ambleside, having twice attained a height of almost 1,300ft. The road was evidently engineered to a high standard, usually 24ft wide in the valley bottom, and never less than 15ft in the most difficult sections.

Below the fort the Roman road has its own set of zig-zags which take it into the fields of Brotherilkeld (Butterilket) at 21250115, due south of the farm. But beyond here, the road once again becomes elusive. The observations of McGilchrist in 1919 are not now regarded as sound, and between here and Ravenglass there are only four likely pieces of evidence for its route.[19] The first is an oral tradition of the road being ploughed up last century just east of Wha House Bridge (205009), the second is the present road west of the same bridge which resembles the causeway at Black Hall, third is the fact that the road was again ploughed up to the *south* of the Roman tile-kilns (135985), and finally there is a well attested length running north east from the fort at Ravenglass heading for Muncaster Home Farm (096966). It seems most likely that this section of the road kept to the valley bottom throughout its length, skirting the slopes of Muncaster Fell, except for the final climb to Muncaster Home Farm. It used to be thought that the fort at Ravenglass was built by Agricola for a possible invasion of Ireland; the fort is, however, Hadrianic, and the port is now regarded as having been built primarily for the import of goods and of materials to be sent by post — which is the implication of its position at the end of an itinerary route.

Two questions still remain; why was such a difficult road ever built, and why, as far as we know, were there never any Roman roads south of this line? Southern Cumbria in Roman times, compared with, say, the Carlisle area, was certainly very sparsely populated, and held no attractions for the Romans in either strategic or economic terms, it is therefore likely that they built this strategic road with its strong forts in order to isolate the few Britons who lived in the area. The fact that the Romans apparently left the whole of southern Cumbria entirely unoccupied

Roman road near Greystoke (425295)

when it was so close to their northern frontier, attests to its almost total lack of importance to them.

2.5   Old Penrith to Papcastle

The start of this more northerly route through the Lake District was first described by John Horsley as long ago as 1732, and in detail by Thomas West in his *Guide to the Lakes* of 1778, and yet it was almost forgotten until Richard Bellhouse 'rediscovered' it in 1952.[20]

Its first section as far as the camps at Troutbeck is fairly clear, both on the map and at various places on the ground. Leaving the fort at Old Penrith, it crosses the Petteril, and heads south-westwards on a direct line for Great Mell Fell. (Fig 2.7d) It

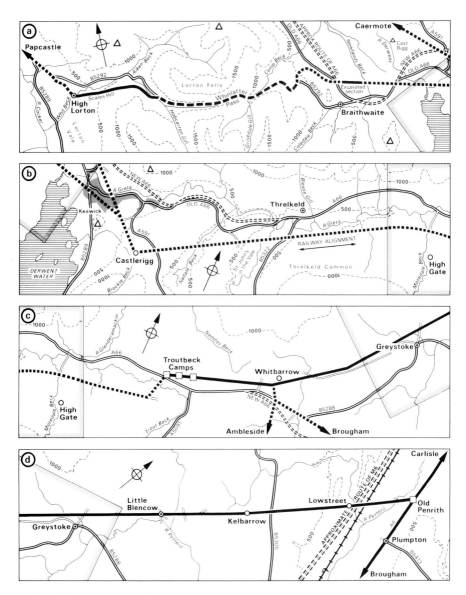

Fig 2.7   Old Penrith to Papcastle

Whinlatter Pass. The Roman line along Scales Hill takes a different route to the modern main road on the opposite side of the valley

then passes a farm called Lowstreet (484369), and can be seen at Kelbarrow (466347) as part of a cart-road. Beyond Little Blencow the modern lane to Greystoke has destroyed the Roman causeway, however, beyond Greystoke the causeway is visible for two miles, running parallel to the present road but just a hundred yards or so to the north-west of it. Bellhouse described it as being 'eighteen feet wide, well cambered and kerbed with large stones' (425295). It crosses the modern road at 418289 and disappears beneath ploughed fields before it changes direction at Whitbarrow, to run parallel to the old A66. It is possible that there was a road junction here with one road leading back to Brougham, more or less along the present A66 (note the Highgate place-name at 444275), and another leading to the south (see below).

The main route continues to the Roman fort and the camps at Troutbeck, but at that point it is lost, and all attempts to trace its route further have so far proved fruitless. One possibility is that the route in fact went no further, but this is unlikely for 'both strategy and topography suggest that the Romans should have had a fort [at Keswick]',[21] and indeed there is an isolated section of road just beyond Keswick. Anyone studying sheets NY22 and NY32 of the 1:25,000 map can spend several happy hours searching for possible alignments. There is the question of where the road crossed the Trout Beck — perhaps at the Gillhead ford near the forts (380270); there is another street place-name of Highgate at 358258, and the two-mile long straight section of the old railway line might have been built along the line of the road. If this alignment is continued to the west for a further 2½ miles, it leads directly to Castlerigg which might yet prove to be the site of the Roman fort in the Keswick area.

The short known length of Roman road beyond Keswick (235242) is also aligned back to the Castlerigg area, and in the other direction it evidently ascended the Whinlatter Pass by a steep route to the north of the present road through Braithwaite. On the western side of the pass it leaves the modern main road at 184249 and descends to cross the stream before climbing around the shoulder of Swinside to descend the old straight road known locally as Scales Hill into the village of High Lorton. From here the Roman road no doubt followed the general line of the B5292 to the fort at Papcastle, just downstream from Cockermouth.

One other road in this area has been discovered; it is connected with the fort at Caermote (202368), and it runs a short distance both north and south from the fort. The former presumably linked the fort to the main Papcastle-Carlisle road, while the latter may have run alongside Bassenthwaite Lake to join our main road near Keswick. The small hill by the River Derwent called Cast Rigg (250250) might have been a Roman signal station, for another Castrigg fulfils just that function near Kirby Thore.

2.6 Whitbarrow to Ambleside

Until quite recently, few serious researchers thought that there was likely to be a fourth Roman road running through the heart of the Lake District, but there now seems to be enough evidence to postulate a route running south from Whitbarrow (on the previous route) to Ullswater and thence over the Kirkstone Pass to Ambleside.

A route such as this is difficult to trace now, especially as direct alignments would have been impossible to lay out for much of the distance. However, it seems vital for the Romans to have had a direct link between Ambleside and their forts further north; the circuitous route over High Street was never engineered to take heavy traffic in any case.

Evidence of Roman roads has been seen at four places along this route; the first is north-east of Matterdale Church (400229) where there is a well-constructed road with ditches; there is also place-name evidence a little further south — namely the farm called Parkgate (396213). Second, a 300yd-long alignment of large kerbstones has been recorded running south from Glencoyne Farm towards a cutting above Ullswater at 386183.[22] Third, there is a massively built man-made shelf which can hardly be missed along the northern end of the Kirkstone Pass, parallel to the present road, but diverging from it where the latter crosses the beck (403092). This terraceway remains on the west side of the stream, it is well kerbed and metalled,

Kirkstone Pass. The terrace marking the Roman route can clearly be seen on the opposite side of the valley

27

and used to have a ditch on its western side; overall it is up to 24ft wide. Finally, at the top of the pass Thomas Hay observed evidence of metalling stretching over some 700yd under the slopes of Red Screes.[23] From here the road presumably followed the present minor road direct to the fort at Ambleside.

Clearly such a route still awaits full verification in the field; there is once again much scope for amateur fieldwork. It is interesting to note that a thirteenth-century charter twice refers to the 'great Kirkstone road' (*magna via Kirkestain*), and as there was little or no road building in the middle ages, this reference suggests very strongly that there was an engineered (ie Roman) road over Kirkstone.[24]

2.7   Eastern Approaches

We have already seen that the *Antonine Itinerary* shows a road entering Cumbria from Burrow in Lonsdale, sometimes referred to as Overborough. This fort was sited at the junction of Leck Beck and the River Lune some two miles south of Kirkby Lonsdale (612758). Two roads from York and Ribchester (near Preston) probably converged on this fort from the south, and there was a link north-westwards to Watercrook probably running through Whittington, and Hutton Roof, and thence using the gap between Newbiggin Crags and Scout Hill. This route lies outside our area, but once again most of its precise route is unknown, and anyone interested in tracing it should consult the one article so far written.[25] Even more obscure is the possibility of a direct link from Watercrook back to Lancaster, perhaps running through Hincaster where, although no fort is known, there have been substantial finds of Roman pottery.

However, the route from Burrow northwards can easily be traced on the map; it runs almost exactly due north, passing the fort about a mile to the east. It has been sectioned at Casterton, and the present A683 joins it at 623825. It is present as a minor road most of the way north from Sedbergh, following the east side of the Lune gorge as an attractive narrow road to the fort at Low Borrow Bridge (609013). There was a link from here back to Watercrook; from the fort it ascended Borrowdale for three-quarters of a mile and then struck out across the moorland of

Lune Gorge. The Roman road can be seen on the opposite side of the valley to the railway and the M6

28

Whinfell reaching a height of 1,340ft, and then generally following the twisting but none the less direct lane past Borrans, (560979), probably crossing the river below Meal Bank (534952) heading inexorably for Watercrook.[26]

From Low Borrow Bridge, the main road north continued to Brougham, making the first attempt at the crossing of Shap Fell, a route to be taken in turn by a later road and turnpike through Shap itself, and then by the railway and motorway. Although all four routes tackle the crossing in very different ways (indeed the A6 ascends from the valley of the Kent), they all lie within two miles of each other on Crosby Ravensworth Fell, some three miles to the south of the village of the same name.

The Roman route follows the present main road for almost a mile before fording the Lune at 612029 and Birk Beck at 609052 (Fig 2.8).[27] The Lune is wide and shallow at the fording point, so the Roman engineers evidently saw no reason to avoid crossing it; they could easily have avoided crossing it at all by keeping to the west bank. The road then makes a gentle ascent of the fell; much of its course has been obliterated by the construction of the M6 and its Service Station, but at 605069 the *agger* is quite obvious, up to 21ft wide with deep side ditches. It is then followed by a footpath as far as the summit on Coalpit Hill at a height of about 1,150ft. (the ascent amounts to only 550ft in four miles.) Just before the summit is

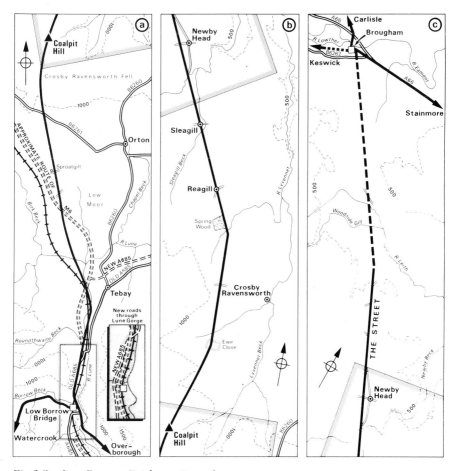

Fig 2.8   Low Borrow Bridge to Brougham

The agger *of the Roman road north of Tebay Service Station (605069)*

The Roman road heading across open moorland on the ascent of Crosby Ravensworth Fell

reached, however, the road takes a turn to the east, presumably in order to pass close to what must have been an important British settlement at Ewe Close (609135); the road here can be seen as a strip of finer turf. Beyond the old village its course is less clear until a new alignment is taken up at Spring Wood (608166) which is maintained for 5¼ miles; much of it is still used as a road (indeed part of it is called *The Street*). A final slight change in direction of only a few degrees occurs at 572244, which takes the road directly towards Brougham, still some 3½ miles

The Roman road on the summit of Coalpit Hill

distant. Most of this last section cannot be traced on the ground until it is joined by a minor road for the last three quarters of a mile. The extent of the fort is still very clear, even though the whole site is overshadowed by the Norman castle built partly over its northern ramparts.

If the road from Lancashire to Brougham was probably the first to be constructed into this area, the linking road over Stainmore from Yorkshire was ultimately to prove an altogether better route. It is described in two of the *Antonine Itineraries* which differ only in giving different stopping places between Brough and Carlisle:[28]

Iter II	Itinerary Roman Miles	Actual Statute Miles	
Lavatris			Bowes
	14	14	
Verteris			Brough
	13	13	
Brovonacis			Kirkby Thore
	13	14	
Voreda			Old Penrith
	13	13	
Luguvallo			Carlisle
Iter V			
Levatris			Bowes
	14	14	
Verteris			Brough
	20	20	
Brocavo			Brougham
	21	21	
Luguvalio			Carlisle

The Roman road three miles north-west of Appleby

It is interesting to give a brief description of this road from Brough, here the Roman road has been abandoned for a new parallel route through Market Brough, less than half a mile to the north. After two miles the two routes converge, and follow two similar alignments to Coupland, just before Appleby (710189). The Roman route is now followed by the new by-pass for two miles, and is then still visible as a green lane, before it is overlain by a disused railway track.

At Kirkby Thore there was a fort, and a junction with another Roman mountain road, the Maiden Way, setting off north-eastwards across the flanks of Cross Fell towards the South Tyne Valley.[29] It is a steep road in places, rising to over 2,200ft, and it seems to have been built to exploit the lead and silver deposits of the Alston area, as well as to provide a route to the central section of Hadrian's Wall. Beyond Kirkby Thore, our road follows the present A66, and at 620265 a Roman milestone has been preserved. The road then follows a number of alignments to Brougham where the main road from the south was joined.

North of Brougham the road to Carlisle continues along a remarkably straight route, coinciding with the A6 for most of its length. After crossing the Eamont, the Roman road goes through what are now the north-eastern outskirts of Penrith to join the first long alignment at 508325 which is maintained for some 6 miles, past several camps and forts, including Old Penrith. The road has been so important in more recent times that virtually nothing now remains of the Roman engineering save the alignments. Indeed, apart from a two-mile section near Carlisle, the Roman alignments are consistently used by the A6, which clearly attests to the use of such routes for the best part of two thousand years.

Carlisle was the site of an early fort on the road into Scotland, and when Hadrian's Wall was built, a new and larger fort was built across the river at Stanwix. The road just described was of vital strategic importance, but the Wall also had two parallel roads of its own: the Military Way, a late addition immediately behind the Wall, and the Stanegate, a curious road, sometimes straight and sometimes very sinuous, up to a mile south of the Wall, and built some forty years earlier. The study of the Wall and of its roads is a topic in its own right, and cannot be started upon

The Roman road approaching Brougham, now the A66.

The Roman road at Old Penrith. The fort lay in the field immediately behind the large farm at the centre of the photograph, and the road to Troutbeck and beyond led off to the left.

here. Those interested are referred first to the special Ordnance Survey map of Hadrian's Wall which shows all the associated roads clearly.[30]

2.8   North-West Cumbria

Sometime near the end of the first century it seems likely that a road was built directly west from Carlisle to Kirkbride, which can be regarded as an extension of the Stanegate frontier. Its possible alignments, chiefly along the B5307 through Kirkbampton, have only just been noted (Fig 2.2).[31]

This road evidently went out of use when Kirkbride was dismantled (about AD122) and was replaced by two other roads leading west from Carlisle; one was the Military Way immediately behind Hadrian's Wall, continuing to the end of the Wall proper at Bowness on Solway. It used to be thought that the defences ended here, but the last fifty years have revealed a chain of forts, fortlets and watch towers running on down the coast probably as far as Moresby (Whitehaven). The entire coastline must therefore have had a service road, interrupted only by the inlet of Moricambe; little of this road now remains. Even behind the Carlisle-Bowness section of the wall the road has been revealed only when forts have been excavated. A branch road has been noted leading from this section, south-westwards from Drumburgh, heading for Kirkbride and thence perhaps towards Old Carlisle.[32] It can be traced from 256593 to 237578 through fields some 200yd north-west of, and parallel to, the old railway line. It disappears at the crossing of the River Wampool, but it is interesting to note that the modern minor road running south from Kirkbride is almost exactly aligned on Old Carlisle, and it maintains this direction for 3½ miles as far as Oulton (246508). One should beware, however, of reading too much into the existence of long straight roads in or near recently drained lowlands, or in any other area settled relatively recently; the straightness of such roads may be due to a modern rather than a Roman surveyor. There is a road leading northwards for a mile from Old Carlisle, but this seems to be heading straight for Drumburgh, and there are roads around Aikton (275534) which line up quite nicely. The possible route north from Old Carlisle is clearly yet to be found.

This diversion around the low lying lands of the Solway coast has brought us back to the main road from Carlisle to Papcastle, and we can now look at this route in its entirety before going on to look at the various branches. The route from Carlisle to Papcastle and beyond became the new back-up service road for the coastal forts (just as the Stanegate did for the Wall itself), and was evidently the main road of north-west Cumbria. Old Carlisle seems to have been the major military centre, being the seat of a prefect of cavalry, the effective commander of the whole area.[33]

The road is easily traced from Carlisle to Papcastle, for the A595 uses the same route for most of the distance.[34] The first long alignment of 8 miles stretches from Kingrigg (371534) to Red Dial (256460), just beyond Old Carlisle. The modern road deviates from this alignment twice, first at Thursby for about 2 miles, and then just before Old Carlisle itself (271468). The road continues with further modern diversions at Percy Hill (229437) and Mealsgate (213423), the first of these being in order to avoid a hill which the Roman road took in its stride. Indeed, for the four miles beyond Mealsgate the present road only occasionally joins the Roman alignment, diverting from it four times, the last and longest diversion taking in the village of Bothel. Somewhere near Cock Bridge (199410) a road probably led south to Caermote. From Threaplandgill Bridge (166377) the modern road follows the original alignment for most of the remaining five miles to Papcastle.

This then was the main road; from it there may have been several branches which can be listed as follows:

From		To
Old Carlisle	1	Maryport
	2	Old Penrith?
	3	Brougham?
Papcastle	1	Keswick (see section 2.3)
	2	Maryport
	3	Ravenglass (branches to Moresby and St Bees)

In addition there are the roads to Kirkbride and Caermote already mentioned, and the coastal route (Fig 2.3). The six branch routes will be dealt with in the order given above.

As Old Carlisle was the military centre of this area, a substantial road linking it to the coast road would have been vital, but a possible route was only discovered as recently as 1955.[35] Bellhouse mistakenly described this route as leaving the main road just over two miles south-west of Old Carlisle (232440) and then following a line of hedges and rides through plantations with evidence of metalling for almost four miles, to just beyond Baggrow (174420). Furthermore, about 1,000yd of this line is a parish boundary. However, this 'obvious' line was replaced four years later by a much more convincing one which branches off the main road at the hill-top near Pattenfoot (225434), heading through the fields, once again with evidence of metalling, for the summit of Watch Hill (187425). From the other end, the route left the coast road just north east of the fort at Maryport, and was traced to Crosscanonby (069390) many years ago.[36] The missing $6\frac{1}{2}$ miles have yet to be traced despite various indications noted by Bellhouse.

The other two routes from Old Carlisle are noted with question marks because the evidence for their existence is rather slim, and fieldwork is badly needed. It is likely that the Romans would have wanted to encircle the Skiddaw Fells by roads in order to contain the Britons living in them. There has been a long-standing tradition of one or two roads leading south-eastwards perhaps towards Old Penrith, Brougham, or Troutbeck. One of these routes was noted in the eighteenth century by several writers, describing it as a 'high Roman road' or a 'high raised way' running via Broadfield Common.[37] There is a scatter of *street* and *gate* place-names, plus numerous straight roads all going in the wrong direction. Here we are in the remains of the medieval royal forest of Inglewood, and the landscape is one of late eighteenth-century enclosure. It is now difficult to imagine the landscape as it was before enclosure, and one has to rely on the often rather vague descriptions of early travellers and antiquaries.

Recent researches have suggested that many of the straight roads in this area may in fact be of Roman origin; it was common practice for Roman surveyors to lay out minor roads in rural areas on a grid pattern in a process known as 'centuriation'.[38] Here, several roads fit a grid with lines 2,400 Roman feet apart, parallel to the road from Skelton (434361) to Middlesceugh (413397). More detailed research is needed into this interesting idea, for this may be virtually the only evidence we have for Roman minor roads in this area. Of course, the existing roads here were laid out by the enclosure surveyors in the early years of the nineteenth century, but they may well have used lines of travel which had their origins in Roman times.

The second of these possible roads from Old Carlisle may have gone towards Caldbeck; a stretch just beyond is still shown as *The Street* on OS maps (334385) and it has been traced as far east as Millhouse (363376). It is mentioned in documents of 1219 and 1300 variously as a *magnum iter* (main highway) and *iter ferratum* (metalled highway).[39] Whether any of this is Roman, and where it linked in with the rest of the system is hard to say; one clear possibility is that it may have been a direct link to Brougham.

Three roads radiated from Papcastle; one to Keswick already described, one to the coast at Maryport, and the third being a continuation of the main road which probably led to Ravenglass. The road to Maryport can be described briefly; it is on a single alignment, and footpaths and roads follow it for the first 3½ miles. It cannot be traced for the next 2 miles, but it reappears as a narrow footpath just before the fort. At Maryport it linked with the coastal road which probably extended at least as far south as Moresby. The coast road can rarely be seen now; at Beckfoot it went straight through the Roman fort, some 50yd inland from the present road. At Maryport it can be seen for over a mile north-east of the fort, continuing into the town along Camp Road.[40] The *agger* was sectioned north of the fort at Burrow Walls in 1955.[41]

The main road south from Papcastle has been located in only a few places, but if the alignment north of the fort is continued southwards, across the River Derwent, it ascends Tendley Hill (090288) exactly where it was described a hundred years ago.[42] The first definite remains have been found near Dean (080252) from which point the road to Moresby probably branched off — an aligned length of road can be found at Colingate (034234), which if continued leads directly to the fort.[43] The main road has again been seen near the place-names of Streetgate (080222) and Crossgates (077211) and is marked on the Ordnance map. Bellhouse suggests that the road turned south-westwards at 073196 and kept on that new alignment until Croft End, just beyond Cleator (010130); indeed the main street of Cleator follows the Roman line as does another section of the main road a mile earlier.[44] Beyond Croft End the road presumably turned southwards through Egremont, heading for Ravenglass, still 11 miles distant as the crow flies, but there is virtually no clue as to the road's route, save that the present main road keeps a remarkably direct course for the four miles before Gosforth. Even the final approach to Ravenglass is uncertain; Mary Fair suggested a ford at 088972 many years ago, but Bellhouse was unconvinced.[45] He did, however, suggest a possible branch road from Egremont to St Bees.[46]

3 Medieval Routes

3.1 The Dark Ages

If Roman rule had come virtually overnight to Cumbria, then its departure was much less dramatic, and in places some of the trappings of Romano-British culture seem to have survived for several centuries.[1] The Roman legions were probably withdrawn from Hadrian's Wall in 383, but the occupation continued in some places for at least another ten years. The *de jure* end came in 410 when the Britons asked for Roman aid against the invading barbarians, but were told that Rome was powerless to help, and that they must defend themselves. Thus began the Dark Ages — so-called because these were centuries of unrest and invasion, but also because there were few men of learning in a position to record events; our knowledge of these years is thus sparse and fragmentary, relying substantially on legends, folk tales and place-names as evidence. Such evidence is particularly difficult to interpret.

In Cumbria the invading Picts and Scots, coming from Scotland and Ireland respectively, made life difficult for the romanised Britons, and yet it seems likely that the larger settlements such as Carlisle and Old Carlisle, remained occupied for many years; as late as 685 St Cuthbert was shown the Roman water system and the town walls of Carlisle, both evidently still intact. However, new invaders were now reaching Cumbria, these were the Angles or English. They had started to invade south-eastern England before the Romans had left, and in 615, at the battle of Chester, they drove a wedge between the British (or Celtic) peoples of Wales and Cumbria. Little now remains to link these divided peoples, apart from the names of Cymru (Wales) and Cumberland which have survived into modern times.

A study of the distribution of Anglian place-names shows that these new settlers broke little new ground, preferring the lower lying lands around the margins of the Lake District, and barely penetrating its core. The commonest Anglian place-names are *ham* and *tun*, sometimes preceeded by *ing*; ham means a 'farm', *tun* a slightly larger settlement with perhaps more than one family unit, and *ing*, 'the followers of . . .'. And yet the earlier British place-names such as *blean* (top), *pen* (hill or head), *glyn* (valley), and *caer* (fort) are all found in the Lakeland core, testifying perhaps to the continued occupation of this area by the British. Indeed, they may have been forced into these more rugged areas by the arrival of the English, whose name of Westmorland probably means 'land of the western border'.

As if the Roman and Anglian invasions were not enough, two more were yet to come. The first began in about 910 when Viking raiders, probably having previously settled in Ireland or the Isle of Man, started to arrive in Cumbria. They have always received a bad press, mainly because the few histories of the time were written by Anglo-Saxon monks, who would hardly have a charitable view of these pagan pirates. Despite occasional excesses though, it is clear that the invasion of Norse farmers, some of whom were probably refugees anyway, was essentially a peaceable process; their type of agriculture was mainly pastoral, and did not compete with the arable farming of the Anglo-Saxons. In any case there was hardly any shortage of land for such a small population and both peoples seem to have lived side-by-side. The Vikings settled around the coastal inlets, and in the mountain core, leaving their distinctive place-names as indicators of their presence: *dalr* (dale), *thwaite* (clearing), *saeter* (summer pasture), *booth* (shelter), as well as the commoner *fell, beck, gill* and *tarn*.

It would be wrong to suggest that there were three distinct periods in this part of the Lake District's history, for the British, Anglian and Norse peoples co-existed for most of the period; indeed there was a British enclave in the area west of Penrith until the late eleventh century. The mixture was unique in the whole of Britain, and has helped to give the area its distinctiveness ever since. The different peoples not only had different languages and customs, but also different types of farming and settlement, varying from the individual pastoral farmsteads of the British, to the more highly organised arable villages of the Angles, and the pastoral hamlets of the Norse. Perhaps the simplest description of the social changes of the Dark Ages would be that the British were slowly replaced by the Norse as pastoralists, balanced by the relatively limited areas under Anglian arable farming.

If no mention has yet been made of roads and tracks in the Dark Ages, then that is partly a result of the paucity of the historical record, and partly due to the small number of people who would have been travelling from place to place. Both the Anglian and Viking settlers must have used tracks in order to reach the sites of their new settlements, but there is virtually nothing to indicate which routes were used. It is likely, for example, that the Anglians would have approached Cumbria on the three routes from Lancaster, York and Newcastle which the Romans had built; however as we have already seen Anglo-Saxon villages were generally sited away from Roman roads, on the assumption that subsequent invaders or armies would also use those routes. The Vikings, on the other hand, arrived by sea at first, although Stainmore was no doubt also used, as suggested by a group of sixteen Norse place-names (including Augill, Borrenthwaite, Hillbeck and Bleathgill) between the pass and Brough. The penetration of Cumbria by the Vikings can be seen clearly from the forty-one Norse place-names within six miles of Keswick (including the fells around Borrowdale), while a similar circle centred on Sleagill (between Appleby and Shap) contains no less than eighty-four Viking place-names.

Once the settlers had become established, tracks must have come into use between each settlement and its fields and hill pastures. In Borrowdale, for example, each hamlet in the valley has a section of fell named after it; each of these *saeters* (summer pastures) would have been linked to its settlement by a path. Next, each settlement would have had a well-trodden route to the neighbouring settlements, and, as the influence of the Church became more strongly felt, to the nearest chapel or parish church. From the early stages when each settlement no doubt tried to be fiercely independent and self-sufficient, it would soon become obvious that some areas were better suited to grain production, others to sheep rearing, and that any surpluses could be bartered between villages. Here lies the origin of the trading system of medieval times, the growth of which went hand-in-hand with the growth of a network of paths and tracks along which produce was moved. This homespun and unplanned growth of a route network was very different to the imposed Roman network which was devised for the defence of the northern frontier of Roman Britain; the roads of the early medieval period were essentially a response to the growth of trade.

In more populous areas of Britain it has been possible to trace roads which are specifically Anglo-Saxon in date, for example the Portways from Southampton to Northampton (via Oxford) and those in the Peak District,[2] but in Cumbria there is no such clear evidence. Nevertheless, it is certain that the skeleton of the present-day road system was created piecemeal by farmers travelling from one small settlement to another in the centuries around the turn of the millenium, and this period, about which we know very little, was very important in the growth of the whole road network.

3.2 Medieval Lakeland

During the tenth and eleventh centuries most of Cumbria was effectively controlled by various Scottish kingdoms, and by the time of the fourth and last invasion, that of the Normans, most of Cumbria was not regarded as part of England at all. The Domesday Survey of 1086, which is such a vital record for most of England, barely touches Cumbria and lists only a few manors in the south. However, in 1092 'King William [II] marched north to Carlisle with a large army and built the castle . . . and afterwards returned to the south, and sent thither very many English peasants with wives and stock to dwell there, and to till the ground.'[3] The Normans had waited for twenty-six years before bringing their conquest to Cumbria, but the changes that were to ensue were to be every bit as great as those wrought by the Roman occupation a thousand years earlier.

We can trace William Rufus's route along the Roman road from Yorkshire by the castles he caused to be built — at Brough and Appleby — and during the next two centuries other major castles were erected at Brougham, Cockermouth, Egremont and Kendal. Once again a ruler in Britain had chosen the Solway as the border with Scotland, but this was not to go unchallenged and the Scots again held most of Cumbria from 1135 to 1157 during that period of anarchy in England. Scots raids continued into the next century, and all this activity gave Carlisle and the border area a great strategic importance for well over two hundred years.

Monasteries One of the ways in which Norman rule was consolidated in Cumbria was through the establishment of monastic houses. There were twelve in total, all established in the twelfth century, and all situated around the Lakeland core[4] (Fig 3.1). Indeed the history of their foundation reflects the changes in monasticism in general, with a move towards stricter regimes and more isolated locations.

Wetheral	Benedictine	1106
St Bees	Benedictine	1120
Carlisle	Augustinian	1125
Furness	Cistercian	1127
Calder	Cistercian	1135
Holm Cultram	Cistercian	1150
Conishead	Augustinian	1154 (1181?)
Lanercost	Augustinian	1166
Cartmel	Augustinian	1190
Seton	Nuns (Benedictine)	1190s
Shap	Premonstratensian	1199
Armathwaite	Nuns (Benedictine)	by 1200

Not only did these houses have lands nearby, but they also had granges and estates further afield. Furness was the largest (in terms of the number of monks and of

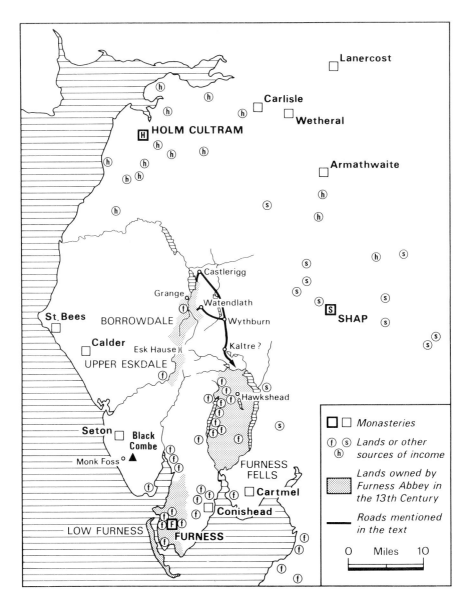

Fig 3.1   Cumbrian Monasteries (twelfth century)

income), and its principal estates were in Low and High Furness (Fig 3.1). The monks acquired most of Borrowdale in 1209, and in order to have an estate between there and the abbey, they obtained the farm of Brotherilkeld and much of Upper Eskdale in 1242.[5] The monasteries were large scale farming and trading units; in Cumbria the production of sheep and wool was the mainstay of their economies. Transporting goods from one part of the estate to another must have been vital, for example there must have been a good line of communication between Furness's principal market town of Dalton, and the centre of the High Furness estates at Hawkshead. When the Furness Fells were divided between Furness Abbey and the Baron of Kendall in 1195, the monks were granted 'free passage and transit to them and all their goods by the way which leads from the

Furness Abbey – the most important religious house in Cumbria

The Monk's Hall at Hawkshead, Furness Abbey's market town in High Furness

The double bridge at Grange in Borrowdale, one of Furness Abbey's remotest estates

Abbey of Furness through the midst of Ulverston and so through the midst of Craikslith as far as the fishery of the Craic and so to their lands.' A second higher road went from the abbot's 'land of Merton' (240771), then across to the 'metes of Ulverston' and so to Lowick Bridge and High Furness. A pack-horse bridge called the Devil's Bridge still survives near Horrace Farm at 257797.

One reason why Furness was the second wealthiest Cistercian house in Britain (after Fountains) was that it profited from iron-making on its lands; good deposits of iron ore were to be found near Dalton, and these were evidently taken up to High Furness where charcoal, which was bulky and difficult to transport, was available in abundance. Furness Abbey was in a particularly remote spot; in a petition from the abbot to Henry IV, the abbey is described as *'assis en une isle'* (situated on an island) and indeed the usual route between Furness and the rest of England was across the sands of Morecambe Bay (see Chapter 5). The extent of the abbey's commerce can be seen from the fact that it had land in both York and Boston (Lincolnshire), no doubt in connection with the wool trade.

With their far flung interests, most of the abbey records mention specific roads which they used; Holm Cultram had rights to dig iron ore in Coupland, to take dead wood in Allerdale and to work a forge near Lorton; furthermore one of their charters mentions the 'ordinary road through Bassenthwaite' in about 1317. It even owned houses in the port of Hartlepool for the export of wool. Furness Abbey's cattle were granted free passage on the road from Ashness Beck to Castlerigg, Shoulthwaite, Smaithwaite, Wythburn and 'Kaltre' (perhaps Kelbarrow near Grasmere, which would have led towards Red Bank and the High Furness estates). They also used a higher level route from Borrowdale direct to Wythburn via Harrop Tarn and Watendlath.[6] It is hardly surprising, therefore, that the maintenance of

The 'Monk's Bridge' north of Calder Abbey

The Monk's Road between Calder Abbey and Calder Bridge

roads and in particular of bridges was regarded as a pious act. There are several references to the granting of indulgences for work on bridges, but there is also the rare example of forty days of remitted penances promised by Bishop Welton in 1354 for anyone working on a boggy stretch of road at the appropriately named spot of Wragmyre, on the Roman road between Carlisle and Penrith (450494).[7] The so-called Monk's Bridge above Calder Abbey (locally known as The Roman Bridge) is probably much later in date.

One question remains, however, and that is whether the monasteries actually built roads on any significant scale; evidently they built roads close to their own precincts such as the Monks Road at Calder Abbey; another has recently been discovered at Shap Abbey.[8] But there is no evidence that any of the abbeys were ever involved in making metalled roads on any large scale at all; medieval roads made and maintained themselves simply by the passage of horses and carts. Occasionally, a road is described in a charter; in 1433 the monks of Furness Abbey granted a right of way over their land between Gleaston Castle (261714) and what is now Barrow.[9] Its route passed just south of Newbarns and then between Holbeck and Stank; unfortunately virtually nothing now remains of this route on the ground, not even a path or right of way.

Documents   Monastic and other legal documents often mention roads in another light — namely their use as boundaries. There are numerous examples and we have already seen how such references can help to locate Roman roads. The 'King's Highway' is referred to at Kirkby Thore in several charters in the Register of Holm Cultram at the end of the twelfth century; for example, 'Adam ... grants to Holm abbey 5 acres arable in Kyrkebythore, ... two on the west of the howses between the king's highway and the road to Soureby . . . and one on the cart-road from Bothinton.'[10] The Maiden Way is also referred to in these grants, and there are other references to the King's Highway at Carlisle and Lazonby, and to a 'great road' at Colingate in the parish of Distington.[11] Evidence of non-Roman roads also appears; a 'Bredestrete' is mentioned in Staveley in 1256, a 'highway' from Kirkby (Kendal?) to Hincaster in 1237-48, another from Hincaster to Sedgwick in 1374, from Farleton to Burton in 1220-49, from Mansergh to Kendale in 1260, and a 'great highway' in Barbon in 1200-16.[12]

Perhaps the difficulties of using charters as a means of trying to reconstruct the road network can best be seen by looking at a particular example. Here, some land at Newbiggin, near Hutton Roof, is being given to Cockersand Abbey in the 1220s:

> Orm son of Adam de Kellet, with the consent of Alina, his wife, gave to the canons 7 a. land in Neubiging in one ridding with the house which Robert the skinner founded on it, within bounds as the highway of Therscheldegate [? Thors-keld-gate] comes from the wood at the north side, so following the highway to a point opposite the barn of Thomas the singer and on the other side of the road through the midst of the hill to the bounds of Richard the clerk, and so ascending the hill to the northern gable of the said house, then following the fence under the crag to the said highway of Therschaldegate, except 2 a. within these bounds which Hallward holds of St. Mary of Cockersand. Adam de Sigeswic son of Edward released his claim to this land for three marks and Ralph de Bethum, Robert de Hotonrue and William de Neubiging confirmed the said grant.[13]

The roads mentioned so far in no way constitute a complete list; anyone interested in searching out the medieval roads in his or her own parish must first read through every available charter and document from the vast variety of sources available for each parish in local record offices and in published works.

One of the most interesting of these indirect references is to the road from Kendal to Shap which is mentioned in two charters. The first is a grant to Shap Abbey made early in the thirteenth century which, in describing the boundaries of a piece of land, mentions the 'great street which comes from Kendal' (*magna strata que venit de Kendale*).[14] The second, also concerning a deed for an area of land, mentions 'the great road which comes from the vill of Heppe and is called the Stayngate.' (*magnam viam . . . le Stayngate*).[15] From all this, it appears that there was a route over Shap from Kendal to Penrith, significantly not along the Roman line, but presumably further west along the line of the present A6. Indeed, it appears that the Roman route south to Tebay and thence to Lancaster was being used as a drove road for cattle from Scotland as evidenced by the place-name of Galwaithegate (ie the road from Galloway) now known as Scotch Lane, south of Tebay but on the west bank of the Lune.[16] This route is also followed by parish boundaries for most of the six miles south of Low Borrow Bridge (611999 to 599923). The interesting point is that the main route had evidently shifted westwards, and yet it was being referred to as a *Stayngate* — or stony road — a description usually applied to Roman roads.

Very few roads are known to have been built in the Middle Ages; new routes simply came into being when people used them often enough. A more detailed look at the Shap route will be given in Chapter 6.

Towns   If the growth of monasteries was important to the growth of trade and travel to Cumbria, then the growth of towns was equally important, though it occurred a century later. Trying to establish when a place became a town is a surprisingly difficult task. The usual process was that some place would become a market, and would acquire a market charter and then a borough charter. However,

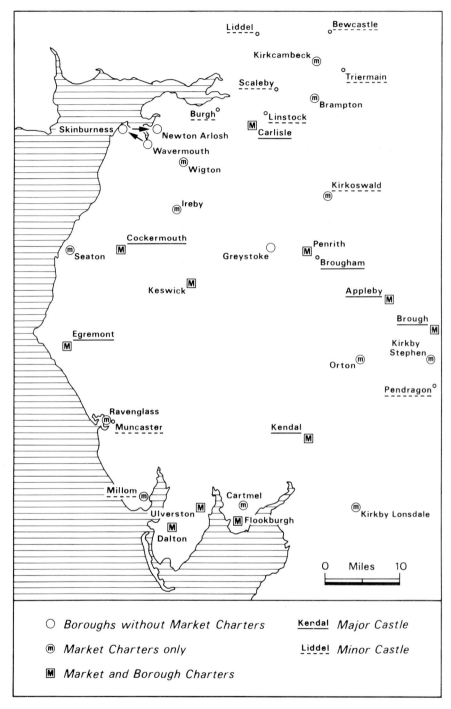

Fig 3.2   Market Towns and Castles in Cumbria (thirteenth century)

sometimes local landowners would grant a full town charter to a place where virtually nothing existed. Egremont, for example, received a borough charter in 1202, but did not merit a market charter until 1267. The prime example of this

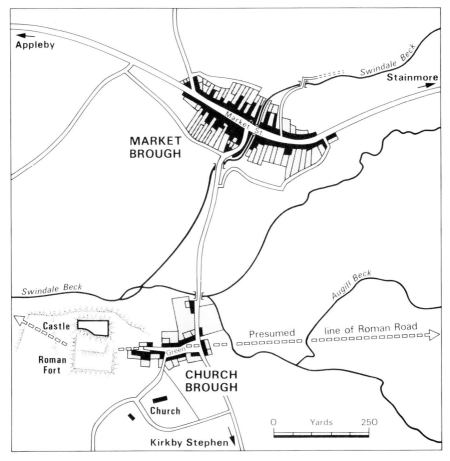

Fig 3.3   Medieval Brough

occurred in 1300 when Edward I allowed the Abbot of Holm Cultram to create a free borough at Wavermouth. A year later the charter was transferred to Skinburness (127559), and in 1305 to Newton Arlosh (199552) with a total lack of success each time; now even the name of Wavermouth has disappeared from the map!

The earliest recognisable town was clearly Carlisle, followed by Appleby which was regarded as the administrative centre of Westmorland early in the twelfth century, but only Kendal was added to this list before 1200. The thirteenth century saw the creation of a further twenty markets in Cumbria, and full borough status was eventually achieved by eleven (excluding the Holm Cultram trio!)[17] (Fig 3.2). What is very clear from the distribution of these towns is how many of them are on or close to either Roman roads or the coast, and that only Keswick is in what is now regarded as the Lake District. It should also be borne in mind that none of these towns became very large in medieval times — Carlisle probably never had more than 2,000 people.

Medieval towns often came into being for military or defensive reasons, but whether they grew or declined depended ultimately on their location as trading centres. Thus it is usually clear that those markets which failed to become boroughs were either in areas which could not support enough trade, or were not well placed with regard to the road system. Indeed, a place need not have been far

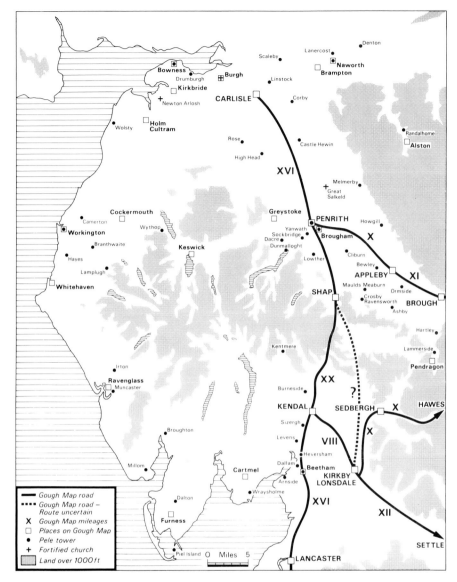

Fig 3.4 Pele Towers and Gough Map routes (fourteenth century)

from a road to fail as a town. A perfect example can be seen at Brough where the original town with its castle and church on the site of the old Roman fort failed to prosper, and a new town grew on the medieval diversion of the road from Appleby to Stainmore, barely half a mile to the north[18] (Fig 3.3). Planting a town was thus different from planting a hedge; a hedge might grow anywhere, but the success of a town depended very much on its geographical position.

Trade of all kinds was beginning to flourish in Cumbria through the thirteenth century; the local supplies of wool and the invention of the fulling mill in the early part of the century (which needed the water power sites so easily available in Cumbria) both seem to have encouraged the growth of a local cloth industry, and Kendal soon became the collecting centre for woollen cloth made throughout the area. Mining and quarrying were becoming more important — coal, iron, copper,

Wraysholme pele tower, now used as a barn, but formerly guarding the sands route half way across the Cartmel peninsula (383754)

lead, silver, slate and limestone were all being extracted before 1500, and the local production of pig iron provided a commodity for sale elsewhere in Britain. Salt was produced on the Solway coast, and transported inland as a particularly vital commodity, leaving its mark in the landscape in the form of 'salt' place-names such as Salterwath Bridge (612009). These have been connected in other parts of the country to form so-called 'saltways', but in Cumbria such names are quite rare, and in any case there were never any roads which were used solely to transport salt and nothing else.

The prosperity of Cumbria was upset by the events of the early fourteenth century. Edward I had taken an interest in Scottish affairs, and, as we shall see, undertook a number of military operations across the border. Indeed he spent his last winter at Lanercost and died at Burgh-by-Sands in 1307. Although there had been occasional Scottish border raids before this date, the accession of the weak Edward II brought them in abundance, especially after the English defeat at Bannockburn in 1314. In the following year, although they failed to take Carlisle, the Scots ravaged as far south as St Bees and Egremont, and in 1316 and 1322 they reached Furness, gaining a ransom from the abbey there but then going on to devastate Cartmel. The raids continued spasmodically throughout the century, and eventually the English monarchs were forced to grant licenses for the crenellation or fortification of houses, as they could offer little other practical help. The typical result was the pele tower with its three floors, massively defensive in construction. They are scattered around the edge of the mountain core — notably in the Eden valley which was the favourite route for the marauding parties[19] (Fig 3.4). Only one was built within the mountains, and that was at Kentmere, presumably for fear of an invasion from the north via Mardale and Nan Bield Pass. As we shall see later, this route was a usual way between Kendal and Penrith; it is given by Leland in about 1540 with no mention of the Shap route.

The second and much greater disaster of the fourteenth century was the Black Death which arrived in Cumbria in 1349, probably reducing its population by up to 40 per cent. It had little effect on the road system — rather it caused a reduction in trade, and thus a diminished need for roads which was to last until the Tudor period, a century and a half later.

It should also be remembered that the medieval period itself was one of great change; the situation in the fourteenth century was totally different to that in the twelfth. The medieval landscape was constantly changing; roads came in and out of use as various towns and markets flourished or declined. We shall see how this affected one small area in the final section of this chapter.

It will already have become clear that medieval roads were fundamentally different to their Roman predecessors; medieval roads were not engineered but made and maintained themselves,[20] and were thus very different to those Roman roads which remained in use. Furthermore, a road in medieval times was not a narrow strip of land with definite boundaries, rather it was an 'easement' or right of way, having both legal and customary status, leading from one place to the next. If such a route was used often enough, then it would become a physical track, but always with the understanding that the traveller had the legal right to diverge from it if there was some obstruction or difficult section, even to the extent of trampling crops. On steep slopes this often led to the development of multiple tracks — the traveller taking the easiest route available to him.

3.3 Medieval Maps and Itineraries

Perhaps the clearest evidence for the course of medieval roads is given on the Gough map, named after the antiquarian Richard Gough, who noted its existence in 1780. It appears to have been drawn in the early fourteenth century and it is most remarkable in that it shows a network of 2,940 miles of roads in England and Wales. About 40 per cent of these roads are along the line of old Roman roads although this figure is far higher in north-west England.[22] However it does not necessarily follow that a Roman road was in use if it appears on this map and similarly the omission of a Roman road does not mean that it was not in use; the Roman Wall is clearly shown, but there is no indication of the route from Carlisle to Newcastle. The Gough map depicts three routes from Carlisle (Figs 3.4 and 3.5); one leads across into Yorkshire to the Great North Road, the second through Kirkby Lonsdale to Doncaster, and the third to Kendal and Lancashire. Perhaps the most significant change is that the Roman road due south of Brougham is no longer given; the route goes instead by way of Shap with a branch descending to the Lune, though precisely which route it then took to Kirkby Lonsdale is difficult to say. The Gough map shows a total of twenty-five places in Cumbria, as opposed to, say, the four shown in Cheshire; this is surprising in view of the fact that Cumbria was certainly less well populated. The reason for the greater detail is probably the strategic importance of this area in the fourteenth century; many of the places shown had licences to build pele towers, and Burgh-by-Sands is perhaps included because Edward I died there.

The map should not be regarded as being entirely trustworthy, however, for it has several curious features. First there is the problem of which places were chosen for inclusion on the map (and conversely, which were *not* chosen). Of the fifteen places shown in Cumberland, for example, only four had borough status by

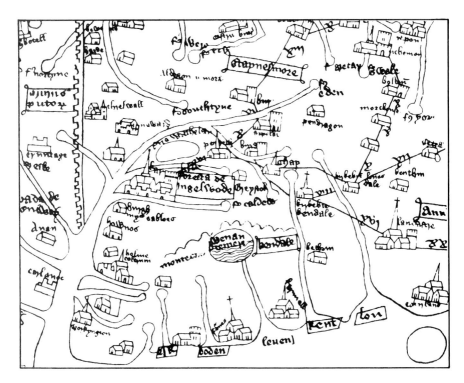

Fig 3.5   Gough Map, about 1360

1360, and yet there were five other places not shown on the map which either were boroughs, (in fact, only Egremont) or which paid more than £10 in the Lay Subsidy tax of 1334. The second problem concerns the symbols used to depict the settlements. It would have been interesting to have been able to claim that these are conventional signs, in a series from the single house, through groups of houses (with or without spires) to those places depicted with town walls and castles. Unfortunately, there is a lack of correspondence between what existed on the ground and the symbol used on the map. Neither Holm Cultram nor Naworth ever had a town wall, Ravenglass hardly deserves its castle symbol, and Furness Abbey appears far more important than Kendal.

Medieval itineraries, on the other hand, are uniquely valuable in that we know that the subject of the itinerary actually travelled between the various places mentioned, and in the case of the king probably had a large baggage train as well which would require a reasonable surface on which to travel. There are many problems involved in using such itineraries; in local studies the main difficulty is that we do not know the exact route taken.[23] As far as royal itineraries are concerned, Cumbria was generally an area where kings seldom came. John visited Carlisle three times using only three routes (twice each); from Hexham, Brough and Kendal. He presumably travelled on (or parallel to) Roman roads from Carlisle to Penrith, and again from Kirkby Thore into Yorkshire as well as along Stanegate (Fig 3.6). One mystery is just where he went on his way from Carlisle to Chester in 1206; there is a local tradition that he visited Calder Bridge, but he is more likely to have gone via Kendal, or even by sea.

Edward I visited this area a good deal in connection with his Scottish campaigns, and as we have already seen he died at Burgh-by-Sands. He also seems to have used Stanegate and the whole of the Roman road from Carlisle into Yorkshire,

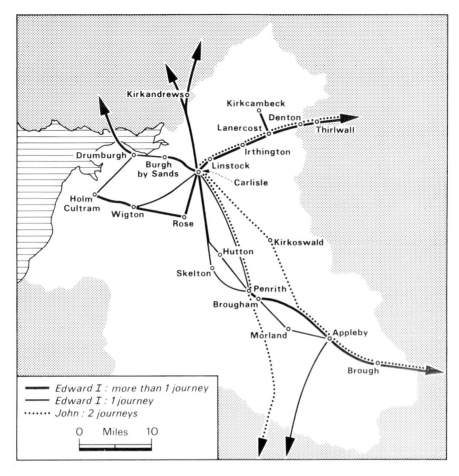

Fig 3.6   Royal Itineraries: John and Edward I in the diocese of Carlisle

Itinerary of King John in Cumbria[24]

1201	February	16-19	Hexham
		20	Irthington
		21-23	Carlisle
		25	Kirkoswald
		26-27	Ravensworth (Yorkshire)
1206	February	14-15	Richmond
		18-20	Carlisle
	March	1	Chester
1208	August	14	Hexham
		17	Carlisle
		19	Whinfell (near Brougham)
		20-21	Kirkby Kendal

though his precise routes into Scotland are less easy to ascertain; in August 1300 he
certainly arrived in the county after crossing the Solway at Drumburgh.

In Fig 3.6, which shows the plotted itineraries of both John and Edward, the road
east from Carlisle seems to have been Stanegate, for John stopped at Irthington and
Edward at Linstock and Lanercost.

Itinerary of Edward I in Cumbria[25]

1280	August	29	Bowes
		30	Appleby
	September	3-4	Skelton
		7-11	Carlisle
		14	Newcastle
1292	October	2	Casterton (Kirkby Lonsdale)
		3	Appleby
		4	Morland
		5	Brougham
		7	Hutton in the Forest
		8	Carlisle
		13	Berwick
1298	September	5	Lochmaben (Dumfries)
		6	'Lambruscayt'
		8-26	Carlisle and Stanwix
		26-27	Kirk Andrews (Esk)
		28	Castleton (Roxburgh)
1300	June	21	Bowes
		22	Brough under Stainmore
		23	Brougham
		24	Skelton
	July	25-4	Carlisle
		4	'Rocheland' (Rockcliffe?)
		5	Ecclefechan (Dumfries)
1300	August	30	Dornoch (Dumfries)
		31	Drumburgh
	September	2-16	Holm Cultram
		16-27	La Rose and Ravenhead (Raughtonhead)
		27	Wigton
	October	28-11	Holm Cultram
		11	Wigton
		12-16	Carlisle
		16	Burgh by Sands
		17	Annan (Dumfries)
1300	November	2	Dumfries
		3-15	Carlisle
		15	La Rose
		16	Carlisle
		16-17	Appleby
		18	Brough under Stainmore
		19	Bowes
1306	August	18	Newbrough (Northumberland)
		20	Carlisle
		21	Newbrough
1306	September	1	Newbrough
		1-2	Carlisle
		3	Newbrough
1306	September	20-21	Thirlwall
		22	East Denton
		23	Newbrough
		24-25	West Denton
		26	Thirlwall

		26-28	West Denton
	October	1	Carlisle
		1-2	Lanercost
		3	Carlisle
		4-5	Lanercost
		6	Carlisle
		7-9	Lanercost
		10	Carlisle
1307	January	10- 25 }	Lanercost
		25	Carlisle
	March	26- 4 }	Lanercost
		4	Kirkcambeck
		5	Carlisle
		6-10	Linstock
		10	Carlisle
		11	Rickerby
		12	Linstock
	June	12- 27 }	Carlisle
	July	27- 6 }	Carlisle and 'Caldcotes'
		6-7	Burgh upon the Sands

An itinerary exists for John de Halton, bishop of Carlisle, from 1292 to 1324. It is not particularly full, the best year being 1294 for which there are thirty references to the bishop's whereabouts. Nevertheless there are 204 references to him being in various places in his diocese; a listing of these would be more tedious than valuable, and the reader is referred to the original itinerary.[26] If we presume that he generally stayed in one place for most of the time between the various records of his location, then at least we should be able to determine the routes he favoured most, even if the result is not particularly accurate for routes covered less often. The pattern of his journeys, depicted in Fig 3.7, is a curious one; of the six major religious houses in the diocese he does not appear to have visited two at all (Shap and Armathwaite), he is recorded as visiting Holm Cultram and Wetheral only once, and Lanercost only twice though it lay on his route out of the diocese to Newcastle. We know that all these houses were flourishing at the start of his period of office; the papal taxation for them was almost £500 in 1291 although in 1318 it amounted to only £66 because of the Scottish border raids; Armathwaite and Lanercost were then described as 'Waste' and paid no tax at all. Bouch notes that Kendal escaped these particular raids, and suggests that this was perhaps because there was no good road to it.[27] The bishop seems to have visited only twenty-three of the ninety-three parishes in his diocese. The bishop does, however, appear to have used Roman roads from Carlisle through Penrith to Brough, and much of the Stanegate which passes close to Lanercost Priory. For the rest, his journeys reflect his destinations rather than the availability of roads; his most frequently travelled route was in fact from Carlisle to the manor of Rose where he built the first stone tower in 1297; Edward I stayed there in 1300.

One other matter deserves some brief comment here, and that is the speed of travel in medieval times, although the detailed evidence needed survives only for a few priviledged members of society. In 1281, for example the Archbishop of York toured southern Cumbria going from Burton in Kendal via Cartmel, Conishead and Furness to St Bees in twelve days; he did the return trip in only two days, and the distance involved could hardly have been less than 50 miles.[21] King Edward I's

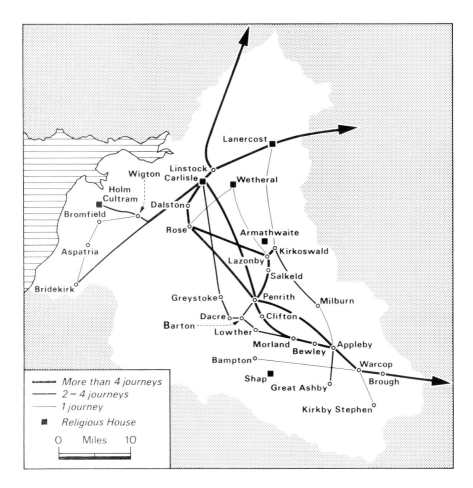

Fig 3.7   Bishop's Itinerary: John de Halton

greatest movement in a single day in this area was the 34 miles from Dumfries to Carlisle in November 1300, and he covered the 32 miles from Carlisle to Newbrough in Northumberland in a single day on no less than three occasions in 1306. His average daily movement was of course much less (about 12 miles).

3.4   Corpse Roads

The sparse population of the remoter areas of the Lake District meant that medieval parishes there were very large, and the dead often had to be carried a great distance to their parish church in order to be buried. Local chapels were established at quite an early date, but they did not usually have burial grounds. Of course many roads saw the passage of coffins, whether on horseback or on a sled, but in a few instances, a route was used for hardly any other purpose, and became known locally as a 'corpse road'. Two of these in the Lake District became so well known as still to be named as such on twentieth-century Ordnance Survey maps, even though they have probably not been used as corpse roads for several hundred years.

The first of these roads goes from the head of Wasdale across Burnmoor to the nearest parish church in Eskdale, a distance of about seven miles across some of the more desolate country in the Lakes. Leaving the chapel at Wasdale Head

Mardale Church, now lost beneath Haweswater (G.P. Abraham)

(188087) the route crosses the valley by a series of fords and then climbs diagonally across the hillside to the summit of the low pass between Sca Fell and Illgill Head. Passing Burnmoor Tarn it descends towards Eskdale and the inn at Boot, on route for St Catherine's church (176003). It is fortunate that the dead did not have to be taken to the mother parish church which was at St Bees! Burnmoor is reputedly haunted by the spectre of a horse which, while bearing a body to Eskdale, bolted into the mists one dark and stormy night, never to be seen again (in the flesh at least!).

The second corpse road to have survived into recent times led from the village of Mardale Green to Shap. The village is now submerged beneath Haweswater, except in dry years when its site can still be visited (476118); the buildings have been demolished, but one of the old bridges still stands. From the village with its chapel, the corpse road climbs up the steep slope north of Selside Pike by a series of zig-zags on to the rough pasture of Mardale Common. The summit of the pass is at 1,656ft and the track then descends into the little visited valley of Swindale, and then by the 'Kirk gate' across the moor to St Michael's church at Shap, almost seven miles from Mardale. The chapel was granted its own burial ground in 1728; the local inhabitants had complained of the distance to the parish church causing 'excessive expense for funerals, and the souls as well as the bodies of infants taken to be baptized are endangered.'[28] The last recorded use of this route as a corpse road was in 1736. But the route itself did not go out of use, for example by 1860 when the railway had reached Shap, Mardale was sending 3,000lb of butter to Manchester each week, and it may well have taken the same route as the corpses of earlier centuries.

There is a much longer corpse road on the very edge of our area — it is ten miles long, and reaches a height of almost 2,600ft just north of the summit of Cross Fell. It used to link the hamlet of Garrigill near Alston with its mother church at Kirkland in the Eden valley.[29] Corpses were evidently carried over great distances from the central Lake District to the outlying parish churches; for example Buttermere, Lorton and Wythop to Brigham (near Cockermouth), Hawkshead to Dalton,

The corpse road from Flookburgh to Cartmel

Coniston to Ulverston and Grasmere to Kendal.

Shorter journeys were no doubt much commoner, the dead from Flookburgh were buried at Cartmel, thus explaining the great number of gravestones at Cartmel Priory recording people drowned while crossing the sands. Even here there was a traditional route for the corpses — they were not taken along the main road through Cark, but along the more direct road, then nothing more than a green lane, passing through The Green (369766) and Birkby.[30]

Eventually the number of people living in the Lakeland core grew enough to warrant the granting of full parochial status to some of the chapels already built, and thus the corpse roads decreased in number. Hawkshead, for example, became a parish in its own right in 1200 and the increased mortality due to the Black Death no doubt hastened the creation of the new parishes of Windermere and Grasmere in 1348-9. Yet Coniston still sent its dead to Ulverston, over 13 miles away, until 1586, and the folk of Borrowdale, despite having a chapel in the valley (established at Thornthwaite in 1240) still buried their dead at Crosthwaite (Keswick), founded in 1175, though before that they presumably had to travel to Brigham, probably over Honister Pass.

All this emphasises the remoteness and isolation of the central part of Lakeland in the medieval period, and furthermore it indicates just how few people lived there; it was the surrounding areas which had the people and hence the parish churches. Between the Papal Taxation of 1291 and the *Valor Ecclesiasticus* of 1535, the only new parishes created in the Lakes were Grasmere and Windermere.[30]

3.5 Roads in The Eden Valley

It has recently been suggested that in medieval times the main north-south route along the Eden valley did not follow the Roman line via Penrith and Brougham, but went along a new route further east.[32] This route is in fact better fitted to serve the villages along the Eden starting at Wetheral in the north (with its priory), through Armathwaite, Lazonby and Great Salkeld with Kirkoswald and Langwathby only just across the river. Indeed Kirkoswald had its first market charter in 1201, twenty years before Penrith. In contrast, the Roman route (now the A6) passes through only the smaller villages of Low and High Hesket between Carlisle and Penrith; post-Roman settlements having avoided the Roman road as is so common throughout Britain. Another curious fact is that Brougham Castle built alongside the Roman fort, was not begun until the end of the twelfth century, well over a century after the castles at Brough, Appleby and Carlisle; presumably because the area around Penrith was not important enough and there was no need to defend this particular crossing of the Eamont.

The alternative road can be traced first at Wetheral; a charter of 1122-3 granted certain rights to the priory between the river and the royal road (*Regiam viam*) leading from Carlisle to Appleby. A later reference to the priory's boundary says that part of it 'crosses the Royal road called High Street which leads from Carlisle as far as Appleby Way.' This is shown on an eighteenth-century map as coinciding with the parish boundary between 479479 and 487474. This map also shows an 'Appleby Bridle Way' which probably linked with an old track through Aiketgate (481466 to 492447). The road must have made for Lazonby where a charter of Holm Cultram Abbey names a *via regia* running north-south through the parish, probably from Scarrows (541398) along lanes to 547388, heading next for Great Salkeld. The final scrap of evidence is a 'High Gate' south of Great Salkeld, (from 550357 to 549348) named on old maps. From these disparate sources it is possible to identify a route which must have been of great use to the local traveller in the Eden Valley and of far more use than the Roman road. The route must have crossed the Eamont at Udford (577305) and joined the Roman road at Winderwath (592287).

However, the growth of Penrith to full borough status during the thirteenth century, and the building of Brougham Castle must have led to the reinstatement of the Roman road as the main route to the north, and the decay of the more easterly route along the Eden valley, to the extent that most of the roads, ways and streets referred to above are no longer through routes, or even roads at all in some cases. This is, however, an excellent example of detailed local research work.

Travellers and Maps 1540 to 1800

4.1 The Sixteenth Century

After the ravages of the plague of 1348, England's population seems hardly to have grown again until after the troubled times of the Wars of the Roses. With the accession of Henry VII in 1485, political stability was regained, and for most of Britain this date marks the watershed between medieval and Tudor times and the onset of a new period of economic growth. In Lakeland, however, a more drastic change came between 1536 and 1540 with the dissolution of the monasteries — for they had been a more important part of the economy here than in the more populous areas further south. The monasteries had been sharing in the growth of the early sixteenth century; Furness, for example, had been establishing new farms (they still appear on the map with the suffix -*Ground*) and the abbey itself was being enlarged. The twelve houses in Cumbria had a total income of over £2,800, but of these only three had more than £170. The first Act of Suppression closed the five smallest houses, and the rest were closed in turn, the last being Shap, not a wealthy house, but perhaps left until last because of its importance as a hospice and refuge near the road from Penrith to Kendal.

Leland

The effects of the dissolution are difficult to assess; certainly there must have been dire consequences in the short term. Perhaps the one bright spot was that in 1533 a 27-year-old scholar, John Leland, was given permission by Henry VIII to search the libraries of the monasteries for copies of the works of ancient writers. Leland and his friend John Bale travelled the length and breadth of the country for six years, their task made all the more urgent and difficult by the start of dissolution. Leland became ill, and his *Itinerary* was the main product of his travels, though it was never put into any sort of order.[1] Nevertheless, his description is the first to give us any detail of a traveller through Lakeland. His route is not entirely clear, but he seems to have gone from Lancaster, through Kendal and Penrith to Carlisle. He gives some detail about the route around the west coast, but this is rather vague. All the places he mentions and the distances he gives are shown in Fig 4.1

Starting from Lancaster, he describes the route across the sands, but evidently he did not use it: 'If I had kept the hy shore way from Lancastre to Cumbreland I should have gone by Cartemaile sand, wher a fresch water doth cum, . . . to Conyhed sande, whither a river resortith, . . . to Dudden sands . . . .' He generally says little about the roads, though he usually mentions the rivers and bridges he crossed. Beyond Kendal (a 'good market town') he followed the river Kent for '8 myles flat nothe' to Kentmere, which he says is on the way to Penrith. We may therefore assume that Nan Bield Pass was a route in common use at this date, for no mention is made of the Shap route. The manuscript then gives a list of mileages around the coastal route — Burgh to Workington is given as 12 miles (in fact it is 28), St Bees to Furness as 14 (actually 32) and Furness to Lancaster as 12 (21).

Carlisle did not impress Leland much: 'The hole site of the towne is sore chaungid. For wher as the stretes were and great edifices, now be vacant and garden plottes.' The entries are jumbled; references to Naward and Highhead near Carlisle are separated by one to Millom castle ('a XL. yere ago fisch was found ther of an infinite greatnes'!). Only once does he mention the state of the roads anywhere near Cumbria in a section referring to 'the way on Watlyngestrete' from

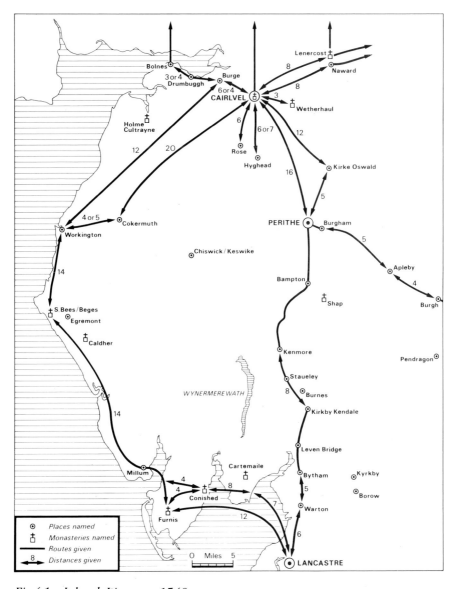

Fig 4.1   Leland: Itinerary, 1540

Catterick to Brough: 'Thens x. good miles to Gretay [Greta Bridge], then v. miles to Bowes, a very excedinge poore thorowghe fayre, and viii. myle to Burgh on Stane More. . . .' This reference to a road in a poor state is in fact very rare in Leland's *Itinerary*, and can be taken to imply that the road system of England in the early sixteenth century was adequate for the traffic then using it. However, with the increase in trade and travel, and possibly the loss of road maintenance done by the monasteries, the state of the roads worsened rapidly, so that William Harrison, writing only forty years later, complained bitterly that some highways 'within these five and twentie yeares have beene in most places fiftie foot broad according to the law . . . now they are brought unto twelve, or twentie or six and twentie at the most.'[2] Harrison also gives a list of the 'best thorowfaires and townes of greatest trauell of England' including a route from Cockermouth to Lancaster (and on to London):[3]

From Cockermouth to Kiswike	6 miles
From Kiswike to Grocener (Grasmere)	8 miles
From Grocener to Kendale	14 miles
From Kendale to Burton	7 miles
From Burton to Lancaster	8 miles

It is interesting that Carlisle is not given as the terminus of this route — for as Leland had noted forty years earlier, it was no longer the important border town it had once been. Carlisle is, however, given as the start of a route into Scotland:

From Carliell over the ferie against Redkirke	4 miles
From thence to Dunfrées	20 miles

William Smith in his *Description* written two years later fills in Harrison's missing link from Cockermouth to Carlisle.[4]

Saxton The sixteenth century also saw the greatest single step forward made in the history of English cartography — for in 1573, Christopher Saxton was commissioned to survey the whole country. He worked alone, travelling around each county in turn, and by 1579 the job was complete. Part of his map of Westmorland is shown in Fig 4.2, with its typical 'sugar-loaf' hills, and fenced-off parks. However, no roads are shown; this is a strange omission, as Saxton must have used the main roads in making his survey, and their inclusion would have made the maps much more useful and saleable. However, for the best part of two hundred years, no further detailed surveys were done, and Saxton's maps were copied and embellished by numerous map-sellers and engravers, notably by John Speed in the 1610s and even the Dutch firm of Blaeu in the 1640s. It was not until the 1690s that Morden's version of Saxton added any roads, but by then a detailed survey of the roads had been published, as we shall see.

Camden William Camden's *Britannia* was the first detailed description of the British Isles, and was published in 1586 after fifteen years of research. It went through six editions in its original Latin before being translated into English in 1610, and it was subsequently issued in versions edited and revised by other hands. It was still going strong in 1695 when Morden's county maps were added to the text.

Camden was essentially an historian and antiquarian, and his descriptions reflect these interests. He rarely mentions the roads, and often the order in which he describes places gives little idea of the routes he took. The country is described county by county; he seems to have approached the Lakes from Lancaster, perhaps visiting Furness, as he gives some detail about crossing the sands.

The description of Westmorland starts at Kendal and proceeds to Ambleside, but then jumps to Kirkby Lonsdale, and continues through the county to Kirkby

Fig 4.2   Saxton: Westmorland, 1577

Stephen, Brough, Appleby and Brougham, describing the Roman road in some detail from Brough onwards. At Tebay he notes two artificial mounds at Castle Howe and Greenholme which he says were erected to prevent the invasions of the Scots, and to 'command the two great Roads'. Which two roads he means is not clear — for there were roads leading north to both Shap and Appleby, the Roman road lying between them, not to mention the road east to Kirkby Stephen.

In describing Cumberland he starts at Millom and works his way up the coast to Ravenglass and Whitehaven, mentioning the copper and wadd (graphite) mines at Keswick, and on to Workington, Maryport, Holm Cultram and the Roman Wall. Once again the description jumps — this time back to Penrith before finally heading in an untidy fashion towards Carlisle.

Throughout, Camden's chief interest lies in the Roman remains and inscriptions; rarely does he mention roads (even Roman ones) and instead he links places together by reference to the rivers: 'And now *Eden*, ready to fall into the *Estuary*, receives two little rivers at the same place, *Peterill* and *Caude*, which run parallel from the south. Upon the *Peterill*... is *Greystock*....' This method of describing the

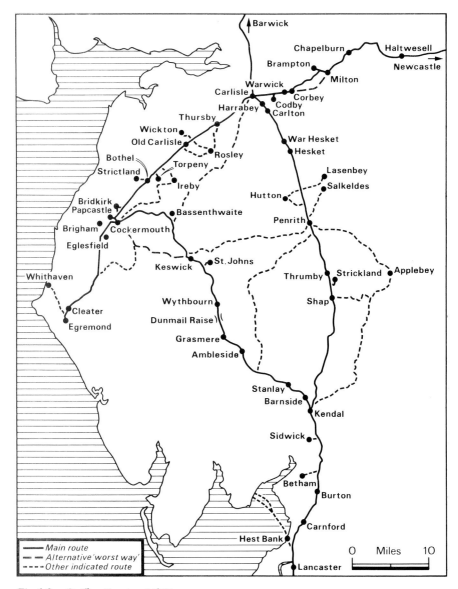

Fig 4.3   Ogilby: Routes, 1675

location of places without reference to the roads is just as curious as their earlier omission by Saxton from his maps.

4.2 The Seventeenth Century

Ogilby John Ogilby's *Britannia*, published in 1675; was the latest in a line of such descriptive volumes, but in one particular respect it was unique, namely that it gave 'a geographical and historical description of the principal roads.'[5] The two hundred pages of text were interleaved with a hundred road maps, based on surveys carried out over the previous six years. There had been nothing like it before, and it was to be a hundred years before another road survey was undertaken. Like Saxton before him, Ogilby's work was copied by many later publishers. He was the first to use the statute mile, and moreover, the maps are at the scale of one inch to one mile. The roads are shown projected onto scrolls, working from bottom left to top right, each scroll having its own compass rose to indicate changes of direction. The roads are shown by solid lines where enclosed and by dotted lines where they cross open ground; down the centre of the roads are dots marking each quarter mile or furlong. Side roads and their destinations are indicated, as are bridges, rivers, towns, villages, castles, churches, woods, and so on — all intended to help the traveller on his way. Finally, *'Ascents* are noted as the *Hills* in ordinary *Maps, Descents* e contra, with their *Bases* upwards'; simply explained, when a road goes up a hill, then a hill is drawn in — descents are shown by a hill drawn upside down!

Four of the map plates have routes entering our area, and these are shown in Fig 4.3, together with some of the side roads indicated. Plate 62 shows the route from Carlisle north to Berwick, and Plate 86 from Newcastle to Carlisle which, having followed the South Tyne, leaves the valley at Haltwhistle, and at Greenhead follows the old Stanegate for four miles to beyond Chapelburn and then across to Milton (556605); most of this section is depicted as a straight road, with little detail, clearly bearing little relation to reality. At Milton a 'side' road is indicated 'to Carlisle ye worst way', but again no detail is given. The main line leads almost into Brampton, then across to Gelt Bridge, to (Little) Corby and Warwick Bridge (over the River Eden), and finally into Carlisle.

The first of the three main routes across the Lakes is shown on Plate 38, this is the final section of the route from London to Carlisle. Just beyond Lancaster the road 'to Hestbanck and the Sands' is shown, and the route itself continues to Carnforth, and along the old road to High Keer Bridge (522719), crossing the present main road at Tewitfield, and on past the Buckstone to rejoin the present road near Heron Syke (529758). At Kendal a side road is indicated to Appleby and Newcastle. The route over Shap has little detail, and what there is is difficult to relate to the modern map; 'Banesdale' is given, and just beyond it are a 'horse house' and a bridge, presumably Hawse Foot. At Penrith roads lead off to Appleby and Salkeld, and the route continues, again with little detail, to Carlisle.

Much more detail is given on the other two routes which occupy Plate 96 and these are shown complete in Fig 4.4. Starting from Kendal the road goes close to Burneside and then over a hill to Stanlay (Staveley); it follows the present main road as far as Ings but then follows what is now the minor road through Broadgate (435995) to Troutbeck Bridge, with its final steep descent, just before which the road over Kirkstone to Penrith is indicated. Beyond Ambleside the road goes to Rydal, and then along the old road over the hill towards Grasmere village. The route continues over Dunmail Raise, into Cumberland, and past Wythburn and Thirlspot to Keswick. The route from here to Cockermouth does not go over the Whinlatter Pass, for that route is described as 'the worst way', and instead the route goes up the eastern shore of Bassenthwaite, crossing the Derwent by the wooden

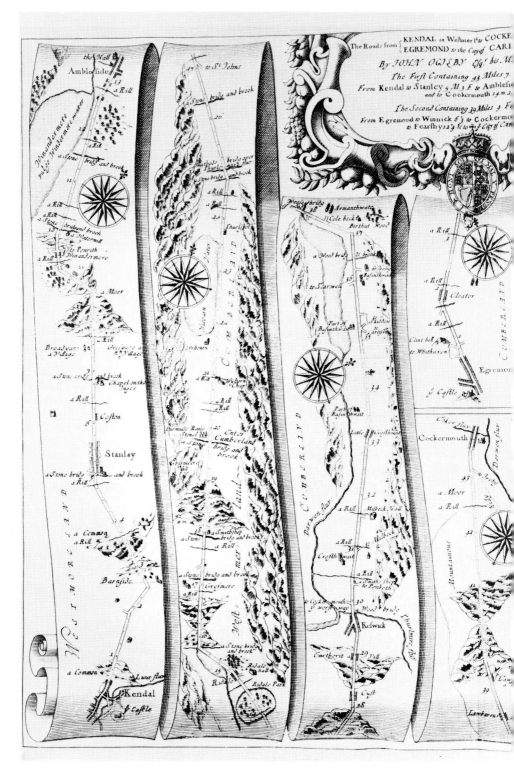

Fig 4.4   Ogilby: *Kendal to Cockermouth, Egremont to Carlisle*

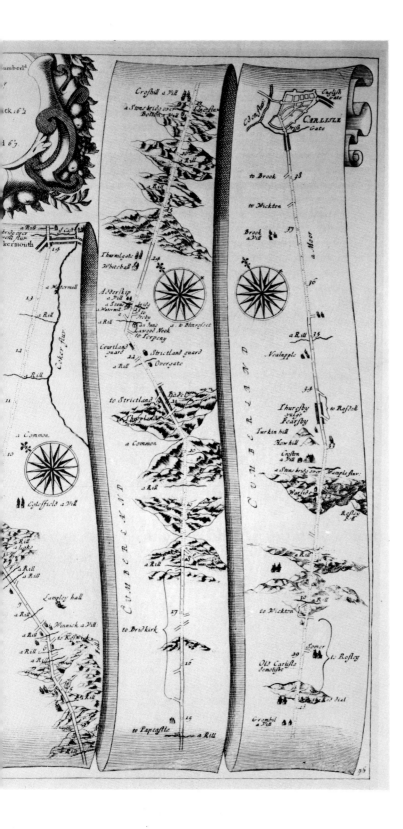

Ouse Bridge. The route from here to Cockermouth is not clear; only two places are named — 'Lowbarcus' (Barkhouse) and Lowfield — followed by a large hill. The most likely route would have been via Kirkhouse (166330) and then over Watch Hill (now only a footpath).

The final route starts in the middle of the same scroll, and goes from Egremont to Carlisle. The curious thing about the first section of this route is that the Roman road (described in chapter 2 and now virtually impossible to trace on the map) appears to be followed for most of the way to Cockermouth. The route misses all the settlements, going almost to Lamplugh, turning north almost to Brigham before finally turning towards Cockermouth. Virtually none of this route beyond Cleator is followed by any road today. Beyond Cockermouth, however, Ogilby's route follows the direct Roman line (now the A595) apart from the diversion into Bothel. The River Waver is crossed by a stone bridge, Old Carlisle is described as 'demolisht' and a total of five roads lead off eastwards to Rosley, the cattle fairground which will be described in more detail in the next chapter.

Morden   Camden's *Britannia,* first published in 1586, was still being reprinted a hundred years later; the 1695 edition is important because it contained county maps by Robert Morden.[6] The maps are essentially based on those of Saxton, by then about 120 years old, but they are the first derivatives to show roads throughout the country. Many of the main routes are clearly derived from Ogilby's road maps, but other routes are shown as well, though only as faint single lines on the Cumberland map (Fig 4.5). Two routes are given between Burton and Natland and between Kendal and Shap. Towards the north-east the Maiden Way is shown, and the road east from Carlisle crosses the Eden at Wetheral — presumably this is Ogilby's 'worst way'. It is not clear where the central section of the road from Carlisle to Cockermouth runs — it appears to go through Ireby (Fig 4.6). The road east of Cockermouth crosses the Derwent at Isel Bridge (over two miles below Ogilby's crossing) and finally three routes are shown between Cockermouth and Egremont, none of which appears to follow the old Roman line given by Ogilby.

Fiennes   The first of what might be called the 'curious travellers' visited the Lakes right at the end of the seventeenth century; Celia Fiennes was a woman in her thirties with an urge to travel (on horseback) and the ability to record her detailed reactions to what she saw. Sadly, she went only from Lancaster via Kendal, Ambleside and Penrith to Carlisle, without penetrating any further into the hills, but she does talk about some of the more mundane details of life on the road, including the lodgings, food, and the state of the roads. At Leighton Hall (494745) she 'had the advantage of going through [Lady Middleton's] parke and saved the going round a bad stony passage . . . on to the road againe much of which was stony and steep, far worse than the Peake in Darbyshire.'[7]

At Kendal she was so impressed with the potted char, she had to go to Windermere to see where this fish was caught, but she found the road to Bowness extremely narrow and not capable of taking carriages, indeed as we shall see in the next chapter, these roads were suited only for packhorses, something not obvious from Ogilby's description of this as a main route through the Kingdom. From Bowness she rode up to Ambleside and then over the Kirkstone Pass and down into Patterdale, complaining all the while about the ups and downs of the road; 'they reckon it but 8 mile from the place I was at the night before but I was 3 or 4 hours at least going it; here I found a very good smith to shooe the horses, for these stony wayes pulls off a shooe presently . . . . The stonyness of the wayes all here about teaches them the art off makeing good shooes and setting them on fast.'

She went on to Penrith and visited Lowther Hall and the stone circle of Long Meg and her Daughters (571372) before setting off for Carlisle where she found some very expensive lodgings run a 'a young giddy Landlady that could only dress fine

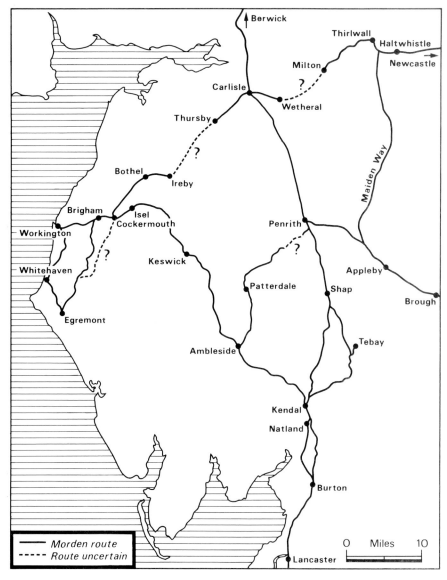

Fig 4.5   Morden: Routes, 1695

and entertain the soldiers.'

4.3   Eighteenth-Century Travellers

Defoe   Daniel Defoe, perhaps most famous as the author of *Robinson Crusoe*, undertook a tour of Britain in the early 1720s, when he was over 60. Whereas most other travellers from Celia Fiennes onwards were interested in antiquities, or romantic and desolate scenery, Defoe liked modern houses and lush countryside and above all was interested in social and economic matters. He was thus unlikely to be impressed by the Lakes. He had barely left Lancaster before he was writing thus: 'Nor were these hills high and formidable only, but they had a kind of unhospitable terror in them . . . . Here we entered *Westmoreland,* a country eminent only for being the wildest, most barren and frightful of any that I have

Fig 4.6   Morden: Cumberland, 1695

passed over in England . . . .' and so on at great length.[8] The way in which he describes the area gives the strong impression that he took fright soon after Lancaster, passed by Kendal (for he gives no description of it) and went over to Kirkby Stephen (he mentions 'Wildbore Fell') and Appleby, thus reaching the Eden Valley by an unusual route. He does, however, seem a little more at home here, and describes the Roman road from Stainmore to Penrith and Carlisle. He then describes the coastal towns and gives some detail of the minerals in the hills, noting the demise of the Keswick copper industry (see chapter 5). He seems to have gone down the coast as far as Ravenglass where he enquired about the pearl fishery (ie oysters and mussels) 'which was made a kind of Bubble lately' (a bubble was an unsound speculative investment with a habit of going bust — as in the South Sea Bubble) — but the locals knew nothing of it! At Workington he noted that fresh salmon were being dispatched to London: 'this is performed with

An old print of the road in Patterdale

horses, which, changing often, go Night and Day without Intermission, and, . . . very much out-go the Post.' Thus Defoe kept to the lowlands as much as he could, and no doubt relied on hearsay and what other people (notably Camden) had written about the central area of the Lakes.

The '45 and the Military Road A traveller of a very different sort came through Cumbria in 1745; this was Charles Stuart (Bonny Prince Charlie) and his Scottish army, who arrived at Carlisle on 9 November. English troops were unable to arrive in time from Newcastle, the castle and town of Carlisle surrendered a week later, and the rebels felt that the gateway to England was open. They marched on to Penrith and over Shap, which was covered in ice and snow, to Kendal and then to Lancaster. They finally reached Derby, but unsure of their support, decided to start the retreat going back the same way, but this time pursued by the Duke of Cumberland who was sending orders ahead to demolish bridges and break up roads. Now heavy rain had turned the road over Shap into a quagmire, and the rebels struggled to move their heavy cannon over this still unimproved road. The artillery fell so far behind the body of the army that the Duke caught up with it, and the last and rather inconclusive battle ever fought on English soil took place at Clifton, just south of Penrith. The rebels continued their retreat, and Carlisle was re-captured on 30 December. The '45 rebellion has an important place in the history of road-making for the English army had had almost as much difficulty as the rebels in getting over Shap, and it was soon turnpiked and improved out of all recognition.

Moreover, a military road was built between Newcastle and Carlisle. It was clearly built for strategic and not economic reasons; and in that respect it is unique in England, having more in common with the Roman roads than with the turnpikes, although it was operated as a turnpike (see chapter 6). Its construction was funded by the government to the tune of just over £20,000 but it was maintained by toll revenue.[9] Construction began in 1751 and the road was

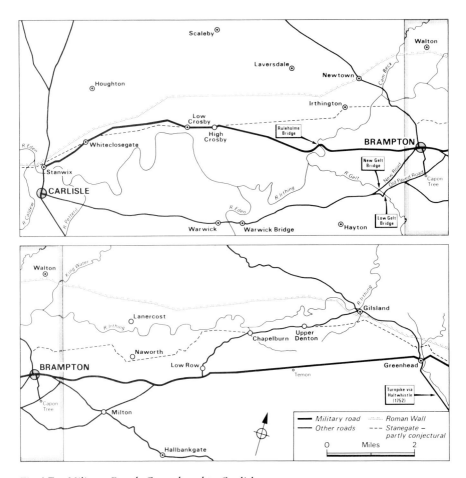

Fig 4.7   Military Road: Greenhead to Carlisle

completed by 1758; it was built on the line of the Roman Wall for most of the way
from Newcastle as far as the central craggy section, where it ran a little to the south.
The whole of this central section from Heddon to Greenhead is now the B6318,
but even before most of it had been built, a bill was passed through Parliament to
repair and widen the present main road (A69) further south between Corbridge
and Haltwhistle. As much of the eastern half of the military road was built along the
Roman Wall, it is unfortunate that the Wall was used as a cheap and convenient
source of material and thus destroyed. In the Cumbrian section west of
Greenhead, however, the road left the line of the Wall and headed directly for
Carlisle for over five miles then on to Brampton (all now the A69). Continuing the
direct line (now the B6264), it crossed the River Irthing at Ruleholm Bridge,
approaching Carlisle from the north-east, the final section being very close to the
Roman Stanegate (Fig 4.7). The new road replaced the hotch-potch of roads east of
Carlisle that we have seen on early maps; although the line of Roman Wall
itself probably continued to be used as a packhorse route.[10] The final change in the
roads of this area came in about 1820 when the present main road from Carlisle to
Brampton (the route given by Ogilby in 1675) was turnpiked, and became known
as the 'New Road'.

Wesley   John Wesley is the next well known traveller to reach the Lakes — he
came here every two or three years from 1748 until 1790, when he was 86. Usually

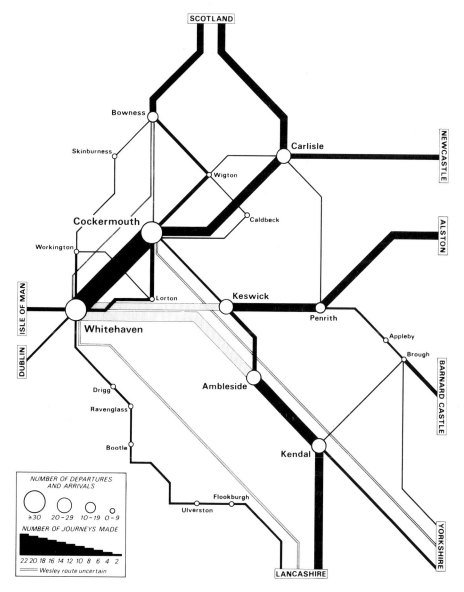

Fig 4.8   John Wesley's Travels

he visited Whitehaven, reaching it by way of Ambleside or Cockermouth, though in 1759 he travelled over the sands, staying at Flookburgh and Bootle en route; as we shall see in the next chapter he thought little of this route with all its difficulties. He seems to have gone over Hard Knott and Wrynose at least once, for his journal records crossing three mountain passes between Kendal and Whitehaven in 1761; the third was presumably Black Sail, between Wasdale and Ennerdale. Wesley was the first visitor to Lakeland to appreciate the mountain scenery, indeed he found God 'nowhere more present than in the mountains of Cumberland.'[11]

His journal is full of local observations — and a wry sense of humour occasionally creeps in, as when he describes Appleby as 'a county town worthy of Ireland, containing at least five and twenty houses.' He rode on horseback until he

An old print of the foot of Kirkstone Pass with Brother's Water in the background.

was over 70, covering prodigious distances, often over 50 miles a day; on his first visit he rode from Allendale (east of Alston) to Whitehaven in a day, and from there to Leeds in two days, staying overnight at Old Hutton (south-east of Kendal). His dislike of the Morecambe Bay sands route was not carried over to the Solway, for he crossed from Bowness over towards Dumfries seven times, only once with any difficulty.

The places where he stayed are usually so far apart and the detail in his journal about the journies so thin, that it is impossible to draw a detailed map showing the routes he used most. For example, it is not clear which route he usually took on his seven journeys between Keswick and Whitehaven, or on the ten between Ambleside and Whitehaven. In the first case he may have gone direct, via Lorton and the Whinlatter Pass, or through Cockermouth. In the second, he may have gone over the central hills, but he is more likely to have gone round by Keswick and even Cockermouth. Fig 4.8 is an attempt to show the routes he used, in semi-diagrammatic form.

Young Arthur Young published the account of his *Six Months Tour Through the North of England* in 1770. He was much interested in agriculture, although he does permit himself a eulogistic description of Keswick and its lake. At the end of his final volume he gives a list of the roads on which he travelled, and a few terse comments about their condition. For the first time we have a comparative survey of the condition of some of the main roads. Not all the turnpikes were yet built, but it is interesting to see that some of them were already in a poor condition. His route is shown on Fig 4.9; he entered our area on the Military Road at Greenhead:

> To *Carlisle. Military.* As far as *Brampton* good; but thence to Carlisle vilely cut up by innumerable little paltry one horse carts.
> To *Penrith.* Turnpike. Very good.

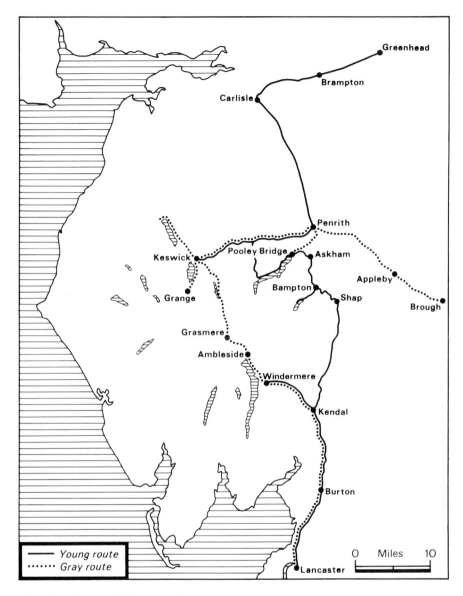

Fig 4.9   Routes of Gray and Young

To *Keswick*. Ditto. Ditto; except a mile over a rotten common, which is as bad.

To *Hull's Water*. Cross. Middling; a coach may pass it very tolerably.

To *Shapp*. Turnpike. Very good.

To *Haw's Water*. Cross. Very bad.

To *Kendal*. Turnpike. Exceeding hilly, and forme very steep, but the road itself excellent.

To *Winander Mere*. Turnpike; now making. What is finished is as good, firm, level a road as any in the world. I no where remember a better.

To *Lancaster*. Turnpike. Very bad, rough, and cut up.

Gray   Towards the end of the eighteenth century the number of visitors increased dramamtically; this was partly due to the improvements in the roads, and later also to the difficulties of travelling in Europe during the Napoleonic wars. These early 'Lakers', as they came to be called, would go round one of the well-established tourist routes, looking at the landscape in terms of its 'Picturesque Beauty' — trying to see it as if it were a picture, with foregrounds, lines, perspectives and gradations of tone to be analysed, often with the aid of a tinted Claude mirror.[13] William Gilpin was one of the first writers to describe the Lakes in these terms; the result is often close to absurdity, but at least travellers were being encouraged to *look* at the landscape, even if in what now seems to be a most peculiar way. If mountains, he said, 'join heavily together in lumpish shapes — if they fall into each other at right-angles — or if their lines run parallel — in all these cases, the combination will be more or less disgusting. . . .' Enough of the Picturesque!

Another writer of the same period was to have a much more profound effect on tourism; the poet, Thomas Gray, made a ten-day tour in 1769 which was to become the basis for those of many later travellers and his description was printed in the second edition of West's *Guide to the Lakes* in 1780. Gray's tour was unusual in that he approached from Yorkshire, entering our area at Brough (Fig 4.9).[14] Here his companion, Dr Wharton, fell ill and the letters which Gray wrote to him make up the text. At Brough, his visit coincided with the great cattle fair, and he describes a crowd on the road as far as Appleby. He stayed overnight at Penrith and then went to see Ullswater which he says is incorrectly shown on maps (many of which were no doubt simply copies of Saxton's maps of two hundred years earlier). The next day he travelled via Penruddock and Threlkeld to Keswick and stayed there for five days. During that time he travelled first to Borrowdale, and was much impressed by the grandeur of the scenery, which reminded him of the Alps. He describes the upper reaches of Borrowdale, but evidently did not go there, and the locals seem to have been intent on pulling the wool over his eyes:

> There is hardly any road but the rocky bed of the river. . . . The dale opens about four miles higher till you come to *Sea-Whaite* (where lies the way mounting the hills to the right, that leads to the *Wadd-mines*) all further access is here barr'd to prying Mortals, only there is a little path winding over the Fells, and for some weeks in the year passable to the Dale's-men . . . . only I learn'd that this dreadful road dividing again leads one branch to *Ravenglas* & the other to *Hawkshead* . . . . For me I went no further than . . . Grange.[15]

We shall hear more of the mines and passes in the next chapter.

Honister Pass is now surfaced, but Sty Head remains only as a footpath.

He also travelled along the east side of Bassenthwaite to Ouse Bridge on the route given a hundred years earlier by Ogilby; 'the road in some part made and very good, the rest slippery and dangerous cart-road, or narrow rugged lanes but no precipices.' He notes that the turnpike from the bridge to Cockermouth was completed, and was eventually to be made all the way back to Penrith.

Leaving Keswick he took the Ambleside road — which was not all yet improved, though parts of it were excellent. Unable to find decent accommodation at Ambleside he went on down the shore of Windermere and then turned eastwards at Orrest Head for Kendal. This was the new turnpike (along the line of the present main road), and he says that all but three miles of it was completed and in good condition. He left the Lakes travelling via Burton to Lancaster, noting the Cartmel sands 'with here and there a Passenger riding over them (it being low water)'.

Hutchinson   William Hutchinson first visited the Lakes in 1772, and he followed much the same route as Gray, adding a few extras such as Dacre, Long Meg, and the ascent of Skiddaw (Fig 4.10).[16] On reaching Kendal, though, he turned eastwards for Kirkby Stephen, leaving the district by the same route that he had used to enter it (ie Stainmore). However, from Keswick he gives an alternative tour which he himself took in 1773; he went first to Cockermouth and Whitehaven (with visits to Egremont and St Bees), then on to Moresby, Hay Castle, back to St Brides (Beckermet) and then to Wigton and Carlisle (visiting Burgh-by-Sands and Corby), leaving the area via Brampton, Lanercost and Thirlwall.

He does make occasional comments about the roads: 'The way from PENRITH to KESWICK, though a good turnpike, is yet dull and tedious. . . .' The road from Keswick to Ambleside 'affords the finest ride in the north of England,' while the Whinlatter route is described as 'an alpine pass'. 'From St Brides we pursued our journey to WIGTON through miserable roads', while on the Solway coast: 'a thick sea fog coming in prevented our going over the sands [from Burgh] to DRUMBOUGH CASTLE.'[17] Like Celia Fiennes before him, he found that all was not as it might be for the intending tourist: 'Keswick is but a mean village . . . we found very indifferent accommodation here for travellers. Nothing is more disagreeable . . . than to meet with a drunken soporiferous Innkeeper, whose small share of natural intelligence is totally absorbed, and who has nothing remaining of human but his distorted image and impertinence.'[18]

West   The number of guide books started to increase rapidly after 1775, but one deserves special mention, first because it gave detailed instructions on particular viewpoints or 'stations' (ie where to look from, and what to look for), second because it became the most popular guide, and went through many editions, and finally because it gave a new route through the Lakes which was copied by later guides. This *Guide to the Lakes*, first published in 1778, was written by Thomas West, a catholic priest and antiquarian, who lived near Lindal in Furness.[19] No doubt he took the word 'stations' from the Stations of the Cross, and the guide often reads as if the whole journey were some religious ritual. The route he gives is a circular one from Lancaster, and starts off across the sands (Fig 4.10). Later editions of his guide were prefaced by a map showing this route (Fig 4.11).

In the body of the Guide, West makes frequent reference to the precise route to be followed, and the state of some of the roads, most of which seem to have been in a good condition, no doubt often reflecting the efforts of the turnpike trusts. Keswick to Penrith was 'seventeen miles of very good road', and from Coniston to Ulverston was 'good carriage road every where'. Furthermore, he says that 'If the roads in some places be narrow and difficult, they are at least safe. No villainous banditti haunt the mountains. . . .' Some lakes such as Wastwater and Ennerdale were, however, rather inaccessible, and were not included in the guide because of the 'badness of the roads which leads to them'. The vocabulary of the picturesque

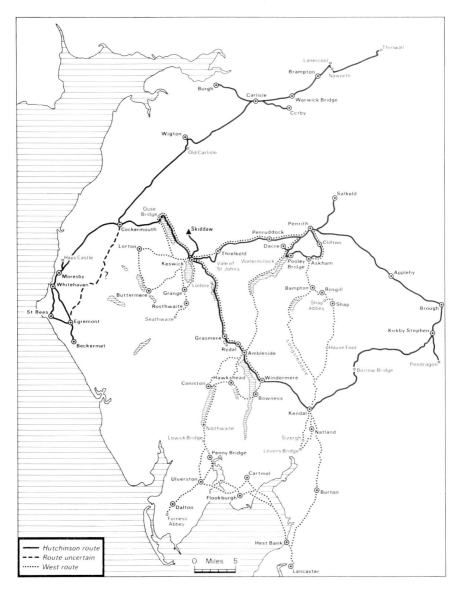

Fig 4.10   Routes of Hutchinson and West

appears quite often, and even roads are described as 'serpentizing' around the hills.

West's view of Borrowdale is considerably better than that given by Gray: 'The road is along . . . the margin of the lake, narrow, yet safe. . . . But there is nothing of the danger remaining that Mr. *Gray* apprehended here; the road being carefully kept open. . . . The road into *Borrowdale* is improved since his time, at least as far as necessary for any one to proceed to see what is curious. It serpentizes through the pass above *Grange*, and, though upon the edge of a precipice that hangs over the river, it is nevertheless safe. . . . *Bowdar-stone*, on the right, in the very pass, is a mountain of itself, and the road winds round its base.'

He even describes the Stake Pass: 'Whoever chuses an Alpine journey, of a very extraordinary nature, may return through *Borrowdale* . . . over the *Stake* . . . to

Miles

	Lancaster
3	Hest-bank
9	Over Lancaster-sands to Carter-house
2	Cartmel church-town, or Flookborough
2	Holker-gate
3	Over Ulverston sands to Carter-house
1	Ulverston
12	Dalton, Furness abbey, and back to Ulverston
4	Penny-bridge
2	Lowick-bridge
Or 5	from Ulverston to Lowick-bridge
2½	Through Nibthwaite, to Coniston Water-foot
6	Coniston Waterhead
3	Hawkshead
5	To Ambleside
Or 4	to the ferry on Windermere-water
1	Bowness across the Windermere-water
7	Ambleside
2	Rydal
2	Grasmere
2½	Dunmail-raise-stones
3¾	Dale head
4¾	Castle-rigg
1	Keswick
3	Lowdore water-fall
1	Grange
1	Bowdar-stone, Castle-hill
2½	Rosthwaite
2½	Seathwaite
9	Keswick
8	Down Bassenthwaite Water, by Bowness, Bradness, Scarness to Armathwaite
9	Up the other side of the lake to Keswick
5	Gasgadale
3	Buttermere
6	Down Crummock-water to Lorton
7½	Keswick
4	Threlkeld
6	Whitbarrow
1	Penruddock
6¾	Penrith
5	Dunmallet at the foot of Ulls-water and Pooly-bridge
9	Water-millock, Gowbarrow-park Airybridge, to the head of Ulls-Water
9	Ambleside
Or 14	to Penrith
10½	By Lowther, Askham, and Bampton to Haws-Water
15	From the head of Haws-Water through Long-sledale to Kendal
Or 5	to Shap, by Rosgill and Shap abbey
7	Hawse-foot
8	Kendal
10	Down the east side of Kent to Levens-park and return to Kendal by Sizergh
11	Burton in Kendal
11	Lancaster

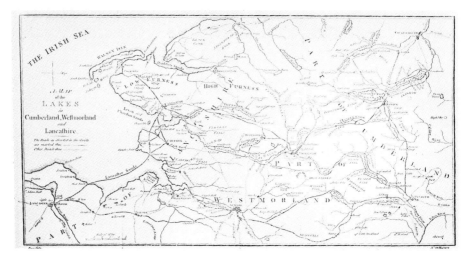

Fig 4.11   West's Guide: Map

Langdale chapel. The ride is the wildest that can be imagined, for the space of eight miles. . . . The *Stake* exhibits a miniature of very bad Alpine road across a mountain. . . . The road makes many traverses so close, that at every flexure it seems almost to return into itself, and such as are advancing in different traverses, appear to go different ways.' He also describes Gatescarth Pass from Mardale to Kendal in similar terms: 'The path soon becomes winding, steep, and narrow, and is the only possible one across the mountain.' On the Longsleddale side, the road was already much better because of the improvements made up to the slate quarries. By way of comparison, he dismisses the route over Shap as 'a dreary melancholy tract of twelve miles' although he does add a fairly awful poem as a footnote, to 'amuse' the bored traveller. It is called *Ode to the Genius of Westmorland,* and is one of 'Langhorne's Effusions of Friendship and Fancy'; it describes wild groves, uncouth rocks, lone caves, awful silences, and is not worth quoting!

The road into Borrowdale (1792)

The road in Langdale

4.4 Eighteenth-Century Maps and Itineraries

Maps The first detailed maps of the Lakes based on up-to-date surveys and not on Saxton, began to appear in the middle of the eighteenth century. Their appearance coincided with the building of the turnpikes and the greater interest in travel, for both business and pleasure. Some maps were drawn for important local landowners, but most were made by commercial map-makers who were simply responding to the increasing interest in and demand for their products. As the century progressed, the maps generally became more accurate, though there was an element of copying which is especially noticeable when a mistake on one map was reproduced on a later one.

The first detailed map of part of the Lakes was a map of Furness drawn by William Brasier in 1745. The map covers the area bounded by the Duddon, Brathay, Windermere and the Leven and is at the scale of two miles to the inch. It was copied (presumably without much alteration) by Richardson in 1772, and was printed in West's *Antiquities of Furness* in 1774.[21] (Fig 4.12) The map shows numerous routes throughout Low and High Furness, and it is interesting to compare this map with a present-day one. For example, the Walna Scar road from Coniston across to Dunnerdale is shown, but the present main road from Lowick to Broughton (A5092) is not. The town of Barrow had yet to be built, and the even more recent coast road from Aldingham to Rampside is also missing. But for the rest it is clear that the road pattern has changed little in the last two centuries.

In 1751 the *Gentlemen's Magazine* published a map of the route to the 'Black Lead Mines' (Fig 4.13), illustrating the growing interest in this part of the Lake District. On this map the 'Way to Borrowdale' reaches Keswick from the north, and

Fig 4.12   Brasier: Furness, 1745

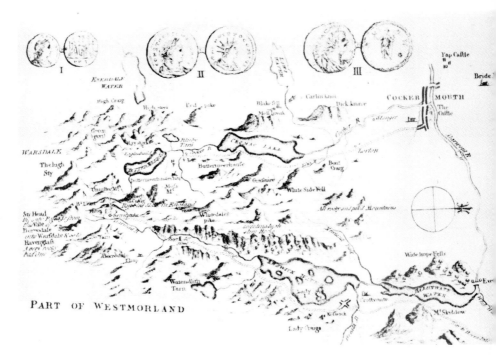

PART OF WESTMORLAND

Fig 4.13   Smith: Borrowdale. 1751

then proceeds along the valley to 'Seawhaite' and the mines. In addition, a road is
shown continuing up 'Unnister Mt' (Honister) — no doubt for access to what the
map describes as the 'Best Blue Slates in England'. Sty Head Pass is mentioned as
being 'the only Passage from the Vale of Borrodale into Warsdale & so to
Ravenglass. A very rocky bad One'. This map is also one of the first to attempt to
portray the mountains correctly, which it does remarkably well.

Bowen and Kitchen's *New Map of the Counties of Cumberland and
Westmorland,* published in 1769 was said to be a copy of a 1749-55 edition, and is
remarkably similar to Bowles and Sayer's *New Map* of 1760.[22] This set of maps has
since become famous (or, rather, infamous) for showing a road running from the
Three Shire Stones at the top of Wrynose Pass direct to Wasdale Head and then on
to Whitehaven (Fig 4.14). Such a route never existed, for it would have needed to
traverse Crinkle Crags, Bow Fell and Esk Pike before dropping *down* to Sty Head
Pass. Beyond Wasdale, the road is shown crossing 'Copland Forest' — before
reaching Ennerdale. This horrendous mistake might have been avoided if the
mountains had been surveyed in more detail. Even the lakes are wrongly shown —
there appear to be four lakes north of Wasdale, and a large lake in Upper Eskdale!
The same errors recur on Kitchen's map of Cumberland (1777) (Fig 4.15) and, as
we shall see in due course, the impossible road reappears in his *Traveller's Guide*
of 1783. All this attests to the commercial competition between various publishers
working in London, who were primarily interested in selling maps, rather than
ensuring their accuracy in these remote areas. One can only pity any traveller
unfortunate enough to rely on them in these parts.

The most important step forward in cartography in the eighteenth century
occurred in 1759 when the Royal Society for Arts offered a prize of £100 for new
and accurate county maps drawn at a scale of at least one inch to one mile. The first
of these to depict part of the Lakes appeared in 1770, namely Thomas Jefferys's

map of Westmorland. Jefferys was an accomplished surveyor who had already published maps of Bedfordshire, Oxfordshire and Huntingdon, and he was to go on to survey three other counties. The improvement in the level of cartography is immediately obvious; the scale enables much more detail to be shown (such as the names of many individual farms), although it was still far short of the standard to be achieved by the first Ordnance Survey maps of a hundred years later. Fig 4.16 shows Jefferys's depiction of the area west of Kendal, with the three major roads

Fig 4.14 Bowen and Kitchen, 1769

leading to Bowland Bridge, Bowness and Troutbeck. The last of these is shown uncertainly just before Windermere; it is not clear whether the old road over Mislet Moors or the newer one further south was to be preferred.

The map is not perfect, and mistakes still occur; for example, at the head of Kentmere the road is shown as going north-east from Overend to join the Long Sleddale road high in the hills, with only this one road descending to Hawes Water. It appears that Jefferys may have surveyed each valley separately without traversing

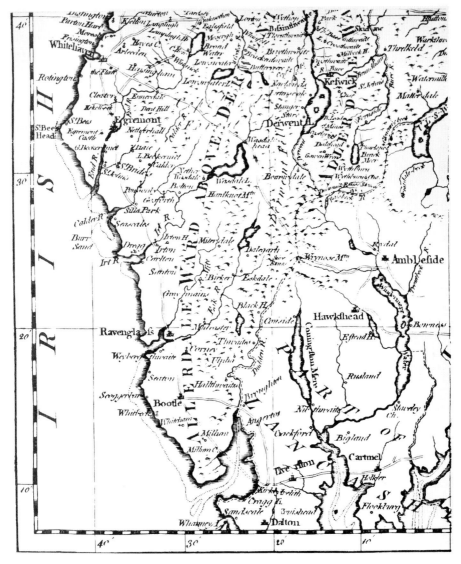

Fig 4.15 Kitchen: Cumberland 1777

the two separate passes. The error is repeated on Smith's *New and Accurate Map of the Lakes* in 1802 and 1814 (Fig 4.17). The second extract (Fig 4.18) shows Grasmere and Langdale; the depiction of the mountains is a great improvement over earlier maps, though they are mostly un-named, and the water from Stickle Tarn near the 'Langdale Pykes' drains in the wrong direction. In Langdale the old line of the road is shown, and it can still be followed from Ellers to Mill Beck (311062 to 298064); from here it is shown crossing Langdale Beck, and following its southern bank as far as 'Middle Place'. It then takes the direct route up to Blea Tarn which can also still be followed as a footpath. A comparison of the place names given in Langdale with the modern one-inch tourist map will show just how much detail Jefferys managed to get onto his map.

Thomas Donald surveyed his map of Cumberland in 1770-1 and it was engraved by J. Hodskinson, and published in 1774. According to the legend on the map it

Fig 4.16   Jefferys: Westmorland – Kendal 1770

was surveyed 'at the request of the late Mr. Jefferys, Geographer to the King'. The amount of detail it shows is similar to that on Jefferys's map, although there are differences; in particular the turnpikes are shown more boldly, while roads across open ground are shown with dashed lines and distances are given between major market towns in miles, furlongs and poles. Fig 4.19 shows the roads leading from Keswick, particularly towards Dunmail Raise and Threlkeld, while Fig 4.20 shows the head of Borrowdale and the Sty Head Pass of which we shall hear more in the next chapter. Donald, having actually done a detailed survey of the county, does not reproduce the impossible mountain road from the Three Shires Stone to Whitehaven through Wasdale Head. These early one-inch surveys are indispensible for tracing the courses of many early roads from Roman times through to the early turnpikes.

It is curious that the first one-inch survey of Lancashire did not appear until 1786, for although the Cumbrian section of the county was remote enough, the industrial south of the county ought to have merited an earlier survey. The

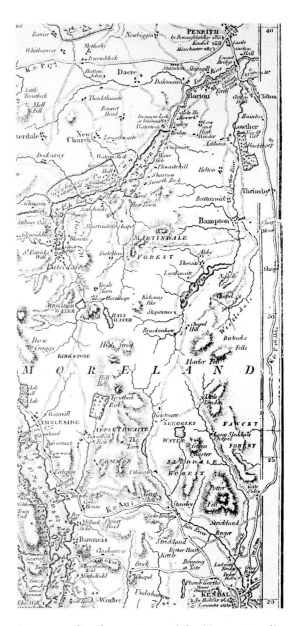

Fig 4.17   Smith: Lakes
1802

surveyor was William Yates, and it seems that the survey work had been virtually completed by 1780. This is the only one of all these maps which has been reprinted recently — albeit at a reduced scale.[23] Essentially there are few differences between this map and Brasier's map of 1748; perhaps the main difference is that the major roads appear more boldly — notably the turnpike from Kendal to Ulverston and Kirkby Ireleth, and the road from Kendal to Ambleside, Coniston and Broughton (Fig 4.21).

Between 1783 and 1794, Peter Crosthwaite, who had already opened a museum in Keswick, set out to survey the major lakes — principally to aid visitors travelling on the lakes or around them to find the best views. His maps are remarkably accurate, were drawn at a large scale (3in to one mile), in addition they show a number of roads around the lakes.[24] Fig 4.22 shows part of the western shore of

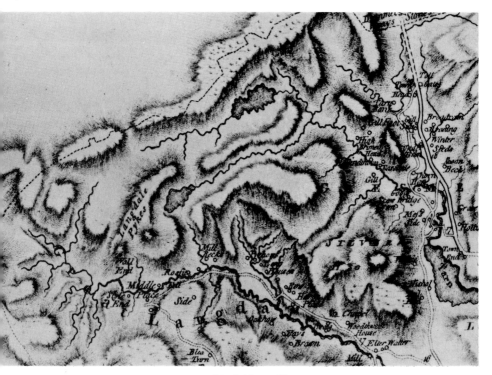

Fig 4.18   Jefferys: Westmorland – Langdale 1770

Derwentwater between Manesty and Hawse End, where Crosthwaite depicts three separate roads. The highest is called 'The New Road Impassable' and this can still be traced as a footpath, while the lowest road is also 'Impassable' — going via Brandlehow. The middle road is 'The only good road of the Three', and is still the route used today. On his map of Bassenthwaite, West's stations at Bradness and Scarness are shown, but no indication is given on how to reach them.

During the early nineteenth century, maps appeared in ever greater profusion; some were merely revised or pirated editions of Jefferys, Donald or Yates, though other complete surveys were undertaken by cartographers such as Greenwood (Lancashire, 1818; Cumberland, 1823; Westmorland, 1824) and his competitors (eg Hodgson's Westmorland, 1828; Hennet's Lancashire, 1830). All this private enterprise was progressively stifled as the newly-founded Ordnance Survey started surveying the counties, beginning with Kent in 1801 and finally publishing its sheets of Cumberland by the end of the 1860s. The hachuring (shading) used to depict the hills is usually so heavy as to make these maps difficult to read in upland areas; the area around the Duddon estuary reprints well and is shown in Fig 5.14. The whole first edition has been reprinted by David and Charles.[25]

Itineraries The traveller journeying to the Lake District at the end of the eighteenth century needed detailed instructions on the routes available, and these were provided in several ways — either in a written list, as strip maps, or as the more detailed county maps already described, although these were not really ideal for use while travelling. Thomas Kitchen produced his *Travellers Guide* in 1783; it consists of written instructions prefaced by a map of the whole country (Fig 4.23). The supposed road across the high hills between Wrynose and Whitehaven is repeated, and the error is compounded by showing two routes; in the text they appear thus:

Fig 4.19   Donald: Cumberland – Keswick 1774

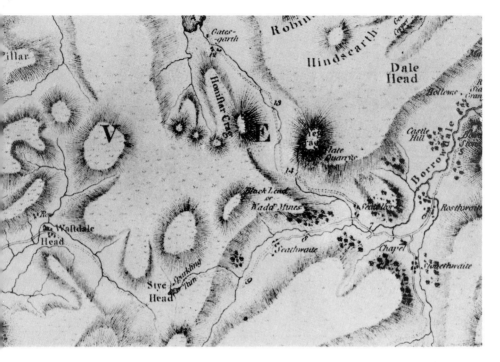

Fig 4.20   Donald: Cumberland – Borrowdale 1774

Fig 4.21   Yates: Lancashire – Furness 1786

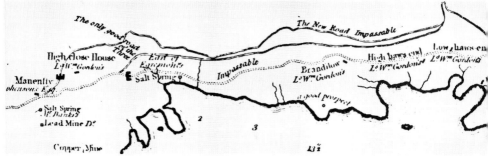

Fig 4.22   Crosthwaite: Derwentwater 1783 (revised 1809)

Fig 4.23   Kitchen: Traveller's Guide – Map

Hawkshead		Hawkshead	
Warsdale	12½	Warsdale Chapel	14½
Egremont	13	Ennerdale	9
Whitehaven	5	Whitehaven	5

From Hawkshead the route was no doubt along the old high road across Arnside, north of Tarn Hows, and over into Little Langdale; the first may then have gone via Hard Knott and Nether Wasdale, but the second is pure fiction. The original text is shown in Fig 4.24, together with several other routes and the other, often irrelevant, information given.

Paterson's *British Itinerary,* published in 1785, includes some strip maps as well as a fuller set of written descriptions. The style of the maps is clear and uncluttered, as the extract shows; here the route from Carlisle to Cockermouth is given, though going via Dalston, Uldale and Ouse Bridge, ignoring the Roman road (Fig 4.25). The written descriptions are, however, difficult to read, and Paterson falls into the trap of copying the details of Kitchen's non-existent mountain route, with almost exactly the same distances (Ennerdale to Whitehaven is given as 6 miles). The contrast between the strip maps and the written descriptions is very great; doubtless he went out to survey a few of the major roads in order to draw his own maps, but copied the descriptions from someone else's list. The only routes given in map form are: Brough — Penrith — Carlisle; Kirkby Lonsdale — Kendal — Keswick — Cockermouth — Whitehaven; and Greenhead — Carlisle — Cockermouth — Whitehaven, thus curiously giving this last stage twice.

John Cary's *Traveller's Companion* of 1790 is a small gem of a book, measuring

The old road from Hawkshead to Little Langdale (331007)

[102]

To *Preston*, Lanc. p. 100. - -	—	213¾
Kirkham - -	9	222¾
Poulton - -	8	230¾

To *Lancaster*, Lanc. p. 100. - -	—	234¼
Hornby † - -	9½	243¾
Kirkby Lonsdale, *Westm.* - -	10	253¾

† *Another road to Hornby, farther on.*

• LONDON to CARLISLE, by *Keswick*.

To *Lancaster*, Lanc. p. 100. - -	—	234¼
Yealand - -	9	243¼
Height - - -	11	254¼
Hawkshead -	13	267¼
Keswick, Cumb.	24	291¼
Coldbeck - -	15	306¼
CARLISLE - -	15	321¼

To Carlisle, by Kendal, p. 100.

Kefwick, though a poor village, receives great benefit from the resort of gentry, to see the romantic lakes and mountains that surround it. The lake is computed to be ten miles in circumference, and contains five woody islands. On one side of the lake is a rich beautiful landscape of cultivated fields, rising to the eye in fine inequalities; with noble groves, happily disposed, climbing the adjacent hills, shade above shade, in the most picturesque forms. On the opposite shore are rocks and cliffs of stupendous height, hanging broken over the lake in horrible grandeur; some of them a thousand feet high, with woods upon their steep, and shaggy sides, where mortal foot never

[103]

yet approached. On these dreadful heights the eagles build their nests; and a variety of waterfalls pouring from the summits, tumble from rock to rock in terrible magnificence; while, on all sides of this immense amphitheatre, the lofty mountains pierce the clouds in spiry fantastic shapes.

The traveller who visits Keswick, will be amply rewarded for his labour in gaining the top of Mount Skiddow, by the amazing prospect it will afford them.

LONDON to *Whitehaven*.

To *Lancaster* †, Lanc. p. 100.	—	234¼
Bolton - - -	4	238¼
Carnford - -	2½	240¾
Burton, Westm.	5	245¾
Cartmel, *Lanc.*	14	259¾
Hawkshead -	13	272¾
Warsdale - -	12½	285¼
Egremont, *Cumb.*	13	298¼
Whitehaven -	5	303¼

† *In going from Lancaster, if the tide is out, you may keep to the left, and over the sands to Cartmel, which is eight miles nearer than by Burton; this road may be also taken in going to Ulverstone, Ravenglass, Dalton, &c.*

Another road, viz.

To Hawkshead, Lanc. *above* -	—	272¾
Warsdale Chapel, *Cumb.* - -	14½	287¼
Ennerdale - -	9	296¼
Whitehaven -	5	301¼

The coal mines at Whitehaven are worth any traveller's attention. The principal entrance is by an opening at the bottom of a hill, through a descending

[104]

passage hewn through the rock, which leads to the lowest vein of coal. Galleries intersect galleries; all the coal being cut away, excepting immense pillars left to support the ponderous roof of soil over them. These mines are said to be sunk to the depth of 130 fathom, and to extend under the sea, where there is water over them for vessels of burden. There are very curious expedients made use of in this colliery to procure currents of fresh air, to guard against the explosion of damps, and to drain off water.

• To *Lancaster*, Lanc. p. 100.	—	234¼
Ulverstone - -	18	252¼
Ravenglass, *Cumb.*	16	268¼
Egremont - -	9	277¼
Whitehaven -	5	282¼

• To *Burton*, Westm. p. 100.	—	245¾
Cartmel - -	14	259¾
Ulverston - -	7	266¾
Broughton - -	9½	276¼
Ravenglass †, *Cum.*	7½	283¾
Egremont - -	9	292¾
Whitehaven -	5	297¾
Broughton -	11	308¾
Mary Port - -	5	313¾
Allenby - -	5	318¾
Holm - - -	4	322¾
Wigton - - -	10	332¾

† *Another road to Ravenglass*, viz.

To Ulverston, *Lanc.* above -	—	266¾
Kirby, *Cumb.* -		
Cross the sands to Millum - -		
Bootle - - -	3	
Ravenglass - -	5	

[105]

At Kirby is a magnificent seat of a family of that name.

• To *Cartmel*, Lanc. p. 104.	—	259¾
Kendal, Westm.	15	274¾

To Ulverston, Lanc. p. 104.	—	266¾
Dalton - - -	6	272¾

To *Kendal*, Westm. p. 100. - -	—	257¾
Orton - - -	17	274¾
Appleby - -	10	284¾

Another road, farther on.

LONDON to *Cockermouth*.

To *Kendal*, Westm. p. . - - -	—	257¾
L. to Stanley -	5	262¾
Winander Mere	7	269¾
Ambleside - -	1	270¾
'Thro' Ridal Park to Ridal - -	2	272¾
Dunmail Rasestones, *Cumb.*	4½	277¼
Wyburn Chapel	1½	278¾
Thurlspot -	3	281¾
Smethod's Bridge	2¼	284
Cust - - -	1¼	285¼
Keswick - -	1¾	287
Crosthwait - -	3¼	290¼
Lawbercus - -	5	295¼
Cockermouth -	5½	301¼

To *Keswick*, Cumb. *above* - -	—	287
Ireby - - -	14½	301½
Wigton - - -	5	306½

To *Keswick*, Cumb. *above* - -	—	287
Ireby - - -	14½	301½
Holm - - -	9	310½

Fig 4.24 Kitchen: Traveller's Guide – Text

6½in by 4½in, which consists of clearly drawn maps of each county showing the main roads exceptionally clearly. There are now few surprises and virtually no errors as the map of Cumberland shows (Fig 4.26). Even the lakes themselves are depicted accurately. Cary repeats Paterson's route from Carlisle to Cockermouth via Dalston and Uldale, omitting the direct Roman route; the reason is simply that the route shown was the one which was turnpiked first. Cary also produced a *New Itinerary* (in 1798), in the same format as Kitchen's *Guide*, that is, it had a map of the whole country followed by a written description of the routes. More detail appears than in earlier itineraries; distances are given to the nearest furlong, and numerous inns are mentioned (for example, at Kendal they are the King's Arms, Crown and White Hart). The names and seats of local landowners are also given, no doubt to impress them by seeing their names in print, and thus to sell more copies! Unfortunately, Kitchen's dubious mountain roads reappear, with the places and distances unchanged, save that Warsdale is now spelt Wastdale.

Fig 4.25 Paterson: British Itinerary ▶

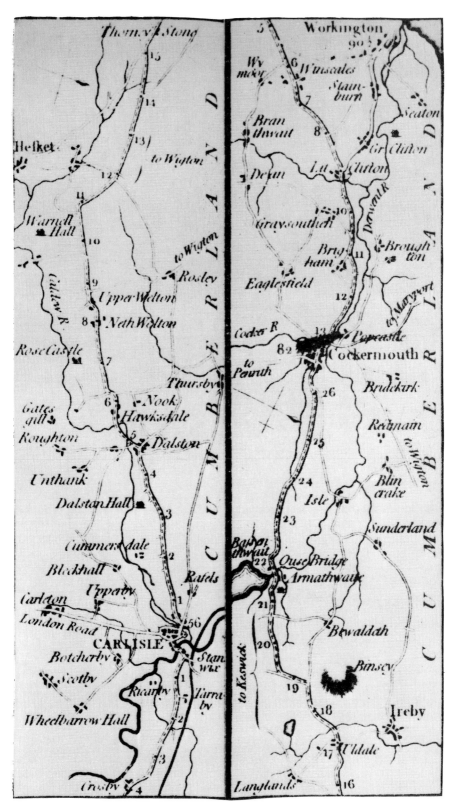

Thorney Stong

15

Hesket

14

13

12

to Wigton

11

Warnell Hall

10

to Wigton

9

Rosley

Upper Welton

8 Neth Welton

Rose Castle

7

Thursby

Gates gill

6 Nook

Hawksdale

Roughton

5 Dalston

Unthank

4

Dalston Hall

3

Cummers dale

2

Blackhall

Rafels

Upperby

1

Carleton

London Road

5 6

CARLISLE

Botcherby

Stanwix

Scotby

1

Ricarby

Tarnaby

Wheelbarrow Hall

2

3

Crosby

4

Workington

90

Wy moor

6

Winscales

7

Stain-burn

Seaton

Bran thwaut

8

Gt Clifton

Lit. Clifton

Dean

Gray southen

10

Brig ham

11

Brough ton

Eaglesfield

12

to Maryport

Cocker R

13

Papcastle

8 2

Cockermouth

26

Brudekirk

to Penrith

Redmain

25

24

Isle

Blin crake

23

Sunderland

Bassen thwait

22

Ouse Bridge

Armathwaite

21

Bewaldeth

20

Binsey

to Keswick

19

Ireby

18

Uldale

17

Langlands

16

CUMBERLAND

Fig 4.26   Cary: Traveller's Companion

Trade Routes

5.1 Drove Roads

Droving became important during the later Middle Ages, and reached its peak in the early nineteenth century just before the railways were built and took over all the long distance movement of cattle.[1] The movement of large herds of cattle on the roads of Cumbria was thus a common sight for several hundred years, cattle being driven to serve the ever growing towns further south. Scottish drovers to England were first noted in 1359, but the trade was already clearly well established by then, as a road called *Galwaithegate* (ie the Galloway Road), running south from Low Borrow Bridge, is mentioned in a charter of the late twelfth century.[2] Drove roads were simply a part of the whole network of roads serving the growing towns and industries, the cattle often sharing these routes with packhorses and wagons.

Up to two hundred cattle or two thousand sheep might be driven as a single herd, and thus their progress would be slow — perhaps only six or twelve miles a day. Overall, the distances covered could be great; it was not uncommon for Galloway cattle to be sold in London, though generally the capital obtained its beef from Wales. Galloway cattle frequently traversed the eastern edge of the Lake District on their way to the towns of Lancashire and Yorkshire.

The drovers tended to keep to well-defined routes with which they were familiar and moreover these routes had facilities such as good overnight pastures, inns, and markets. These drove roads were usually wide (partly due to the effects of droving) with some grazing available on the road itself; in some areas of the Pennines these roads have survived as walled and unsurfaced tracks known as 'green roads'.[3] They sometimes followed Roman roads, or kept to higher ground above the enclosed farmland of the valleys. In the course of time their routes would alter, perhaps because of the growth of new markets, the enclosure of formerly open land, or because of the imposition of tolls on the eighteenth-century turnpike roads. Thus later drove roads sometimes took rather peculiar and difficult routes, as we shall see.

Drove roads in Cumbria tend to have survived as wide lanes between walls; they may or may not have been surfaced. Even if a metalled road now runs along them the metalling rarely fills the space between the walls and the lane often leads out onto open moorland. These roads can be easily distinguished from those equally wide roads created by Parliamentary enclosure after about 1760, for the drovers' roads twist and turn to follow the lie of the land while the enclosure roads are

A typical wide drove road near Orton

usually much straighter. These typical rolling English roads were not made by G.K. Chesterton's rolling English drunkard, but came into being much more prosaically in the days before the roads were enclosed by walls, when the traveller or drover had the right to follow the best route available.

The physical remains of drove roads are usually fragmentary and give no overall idea of the main routes, and thus other types of evidence must be used. First there is documentary evidence, either of roads used for droving, of the drovers themselves, or of those living near such roads. Second there is place-name evidence including the survival of elements such as Ox-, Scots-, Drover's- or Gal(loway). Such evidence is not totally reliable — for instance a 'Scotchman's Bridge' near Tebay turns out to be a road bridge over the railway! The Norse element *wath* meaning a ford also tends to occur frequently along drove routes, including the crossings of the Solway Firth.

The overnight stopping places also provide evidence; they were usually between six and twelve miles apart, and were furnished with both pasture and inns. Field names connected with droving may include 'half penny field' (derived from the charge for using the field), or large open areas such as Broad Field (425445) which were used to provide pasture for animals in transit. Many of the inns were named after some aspect of the droving trade, and some names still survive. However, there are the obvious difficulties that inns may have been re-named, and moreover the number of inns in rural areas has decreased drastically in the last hundred years. Ideally, it would be interesting to scan the local directories of the mid-nineteenth century, but even a quick perusal of the current *Yellow Pages* reveals the following pub names which may indicate former drove routes — indeed all but two of them are on known drove roads: Black Bull (Brough Sowerby, Coniston, Cockermouth, Kirkby Stephen, Egremont, Kirkoswald), Bull (Sedbergh, Shap), Caledonian (Carlisle), Drove (Roadhead), Grey Bull (Penrith), Highland Laddie (Glasson, Todhill), Scotch (Brampton), Tam O'Shanter (Brampton) and the White Ox (Carlisle). All these are marked on Fig 5.1 as is the Drover's Rest at Monkhill.[4] There is even a farm called Drovergate (538322).

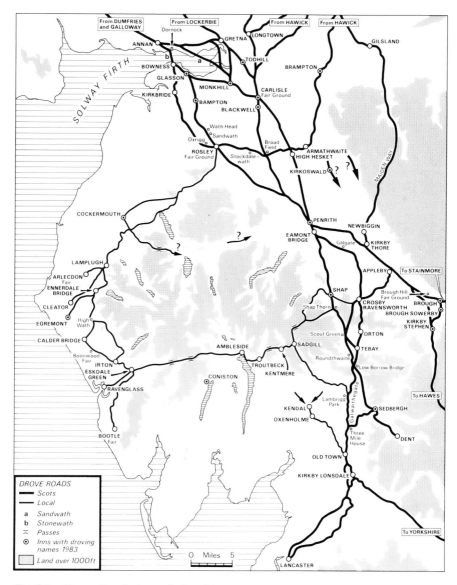

Fig 5.1   Drove Roads through Cumbria

Finally, the location of the main cattle fairs can also help trace the drove roads; it should come as no surprise to learn that Carlisle had a fair, the one at Appleby is still famous (though now for horses and gypsies), and another was held a few miles west of Brough. But the other major fair in Cumbria was held on a largely forgotten site at Rosley, south-east of Wigton. Other towns and villages had lesser cattle markets which supplied cattle to the major markets and thence to the rest of England. There were spring fairs along the coast for cattle which had been kept over winter, and autumn fairs along the main drove roads to encourage droving to continue late in the season (for example at Penrith, Kirkby Stephen, Kirkby Lonsdale, and Kendal).

We can now turn and look at the drove roads themselves; they can be divided into two distinct types, namely those from Scotland which traversed the eastern

99

*Fig 5.2   Carlisle: Cattle
Market and Drovers Lane*

edge of the Lake District, and second, the local routes within the Lakes which linked into the main system at various points (Fig 5.1).

Scots Drove Roads Most of the cattle passing through Cumbria came from Galloway, with some from the Southern Uplands of Scotland, and even a few having arrived by boat from Ireland; they followed three main routes. The easternmost route took cattle up the South Tyne Valley, and along the Roman Maiden Way which eventually dropped down into the Eden Valley at Kirkby Thore, close to the markets at Appleby and Brough. Brough Hill Fair was established as early as 1330, and was held on a small hill some two miles west of the town. By the eighteenth century, over 10,000 Scottish beasts were sold there in the two days of the fair (30 September to 1 October). From there, the cattle were driven either over the Roman Stainmore route into Yorkshire, or south to Kirkby Stephen and Hawes.

The bulk of the Scottish cattle probably entered England at Carlisle. The fair here had been established by the time of Henry I (1100-35), and was held on several days between August and Christmas; up to 18,000 cattle a year passed through as early as the 1660s. The fair was held north of the town on an island in the River Eden. A map of the city in Hutchinson's *History of Cumberland* (1794) shows a wide 'Drover's Lane' leading around the city from Scotch Gate to the top of Botchergate, outside the walls (Fig 5.2). The cattle were then driven down the Roman road, or down one of the two parallel roads two and three miles further west, leading to Broad Field, the grazing ground almost half way to Penrith.

The third route of entry was by one of the several fords across the Solway, a route which became more popular when the roads around Carlisle were turnpiked and the passage of cattle along them was discouraged. On the other hand, crossing the sands also had its disadvantages, especially if the cattle were caught by the incoming tide. Nevertheless these routes across the sands had been known and used by the local inhabitants for hundreds of years. Hadrian had found it necessary

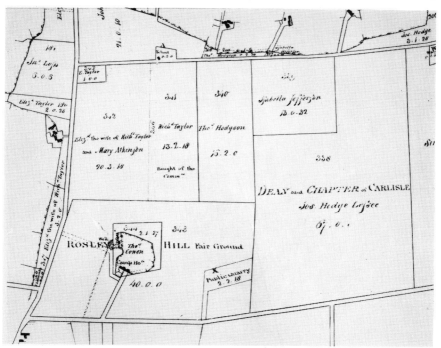

Fig 5.3   Rosley – Enclosure Map

*Fig 5.4   Inglewood Forest
– Hutchinson 1793*

to fortify this coast against attack, and, as we have already seen, Edward I probably took his whole army across the Stonewath in August 1300; further upstream was the much longer Sandwath crossing. Cattle from Galloway had always used these routes, some going on to Carlisle along the line of Hadrian's Wall, while others went south to the fair ground at Rosley (318456).

J.D. Marshall has provided an excellent description of Rosley as it is now, and of the fair in its hey-day.[6] The approach roads still have wide grassy verges, but these are turnpike and enclosure roads of the late eighteenth and early nineteenth centuries. The reason for the location of an important cattle fair in what is now an almost totally empty place is not immediately obvious. However, the fords across the Solway are but twelve miles distant, and in the other direction lay Broad Field (7 miles) and Penrith (15 miles). To the west lie the lush pastures of the West Cumberland coast, and local cattle were also brought here to join the main drove roads to the south. The fair ground itself covered forty acres around Camp House (later the Hope and Anchor Inn), but the enclosure of 1824 has meant that the old drove roads have been either straightened or removed entirely from the landscape (Fig 5.3). As drove roads were not engineered or metalled (like Roman roads), they stood little chance of surviving the wholesale re-designing of the landscape which enclosure of this date (by Act of Parliament) entailed. Nevertheless, the cattle must have proceeded to Penrith where they would have met other cattle coming from Carlisle.

This whole area, most of which formed part of the great medieval forest of Inglewood, and was thus only settled and enclosed at a late date, is shown on the map of Cumberland in Hutchinson's *History* (Fig 5.4). There are several unenclosed roads (shown by dashed lines) converging on Rosley Hill, and then an enclosed turnpike road leads almost directly to Penrith. Further east, Broad Field can be seen, crossed by the drove road from Carlisle, and beyond it is the Roman road.

From Penrith three routes were available — first continuing along the Roman road to Brough and Stainmore, second along the present A6 to Shap and cutting across to the Lune Valley or third, a route in between, along the Lyvennet Valley via Crosby Ravensworth and Orton again descending into the Lune valley. The seven roads which converge on Orton show clearly that it was once a place of some importance. There were several cross routes — perhaps including the use of the Roman road between Crosby Ravensworth and Scout Green. These routes heading south all converged on Low Borrow Bridge from where some would have followed the Roman road to Sedbergh but others would have taken the *Galwaithegate* mentioned in a late twelfth-century charter. William Farrer's footnote to this charter is worth quoting directly:

> The reference to 'Galwaithgate' is very interesting from this curious lane, running as directly north and south as the hills and dales permit, has been used for centuries since the date of this charter (1186-1201) as a driving road for cattle from Scotland to England, and was probably used by the Scotch in their longer expeditions into England in the time of King Stephen and Edward II. When sheep, cattle or ponies were being driven south from Shap the stages were short and the resting places frequent. Between Tebay and Kirkby Lonsdale they were — Low Borrow Bridge, Lambrigs Park, Three Mile House, and Old Town, stages of 5 to 6 miles a day.[7]

No doubt the cattle could have been driven two such stages on a good day. The route can be traced southwards from Low Borrow Bridge. It keeps below the railway as far as 612004, and then it climbs to join the A685 at 610000. It then lies a little above the main road until 607982 where it swings southwards, crossing the main road, and can be followed as a lane (and parish boundary) to Lambrigg Park, although it has been cut by the M6 in two places. In the Middle Ages this route became known as Scotch Lane, and is marked as 'Old Scots Road' on an enclosure map of 1850. This wide lane with its grassy verges makes a rather pleasant alternative to the motorway, and can be followed down to the hamlet of Old Town which even had its own October cattle fair. Here in 1840 it was noted that 'the Farm House upon this Estate is occupied as an Inn, and is favourably situated for taking in Scotch Cattle being upon Scotch driving Road'.[8] But the days of this trade were numbered; the plans for the new railway over Shap were already drawn, and by 1855 cattle droving had all but ceased, the cattle then travelling on the new 'iron roads'.

Local Drove Roads[9]   By the seventeenth century Lakeland farms were also actively engaged in the cattle trade, generally buying young Scots black cattle in the autumn and fattening them over winter for sale in the following spring. This trade was carried on throughout Cumbria, especially near the main Scots drove roads but also in the still remote areas of western Cumberland. By the nineteenth century, cattle markets were being held at places such as Bootle, Boonwood and Arlecdon in April each year and the cattle then taken north to Cockermouth and Rosley, or direct across the Lakeland fells.

The main drove route northwards has been identified, and can be followed on foot from Eskdale right through to Cockermouth (Fig 5.5). From Eskdale Green it followed the present road to Santon Bridge (111016) and then along what is still an excellent example of a drove road to Strands where it crosses the River Irt (128037). Beyond here the drove headed north-westwards and out onto open country, remaining on the lower fells in order to avoid the hedges of the enclosed farm land. The route can be traced again from Hollow Moor (104056) to Sergeant

Galwaithegate. The old Scots drove road, with the M6 alongside

Galwaithegate, now contained by the stone walls (604969)

High Wath. The ford over the Calder

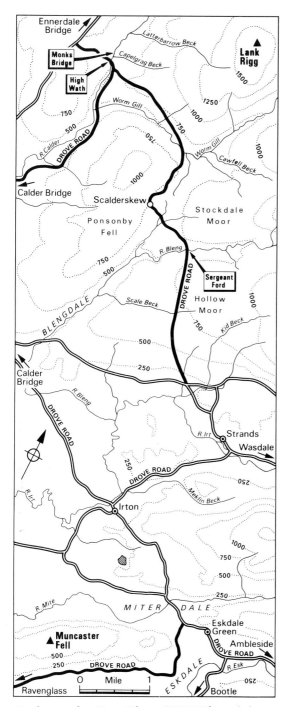

Fig 5.5   Drove Road: Eskdale to High Wath

Ford over the River Bleng (099073), and thence around the edge of Stockdale Moor to cross Worm Gill (089091) and then on to High Wath (ie High Ford) over the Calder (064102), close to Monk's Bridge. From here the drove route can be followed along the largely unenclosed road to Ennerdale Bridge (070158) and then to Croasdale (093175), Lamplugh (089209), Mockerkin (090232), Mosser (115251) and Cockermouth.

The other route taken from Eskdale lay over the Hard Knott and Wrynose passes, already described in chapter 2, and this was the usual route between this part of the coast and Kendal. Indeed the coastal route south beyond Bootle, with its crossings of the sands was 'not much frequented' for the mountain road was described in 1800 as 'a packhorse and prime way'.[10]

The route as far as Ambleside is clear, but here the cattle drovers once again took a more difficult route eastwards in order to avoid the enclosed farmland between Ambleside and Kendal. They took the high road out of Ambleside to High Skelghyll (390029) and Troutbeck (407026); a pleasant walk today avoiding the traffic on the A591 (Fig 5.6). Crossing the Trout Beck, the drovers then took the gently rising Garburn Pass road across to Kentmere and over the next ridge by Stile End to Sadgill in Longsleddale. A petition of 1717 written in a typically breathless legal style shows clearly that this was a major route, but not without its problems:

> The inhabitants of Long Sleddale, Langdale, Grasmere Rydal and Loughrigg, Ambleside, Troutbeck, Kentmere and several other townships in the Barony of Kendall, show that the great road and public highway between Hawksyde, Ambleside, Shap, Penrith and Appleby, very much used by travellers, drovers and others having occasion frequently to pass and repass to and from the said markets with cattle and other goods, in which public highway there is a water or rivulet called Sadgill which by the violent and sudden rain there is often raised and overflows its banks so that no passenger dare venture to cross the same and many times travellers are forced to stay two or three days before they dare venture to cross and are often in danger with their cattle of being lost in crossing the said water to the great prejudice of trade, and pray that a bridge may be erected over the same.[11]

Marshall comments that 'it appears that a small but turbulent river could obstruct the passage of cattle more effectively than a wider and slower one, which could be waded or swum without encountering obstruction'.[12]

Sadgill Bridge on the drove road in Longsleddale

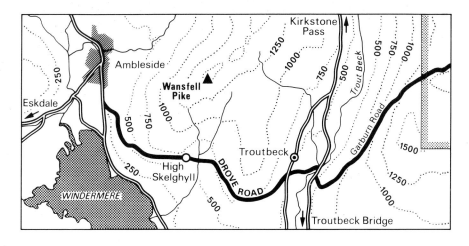

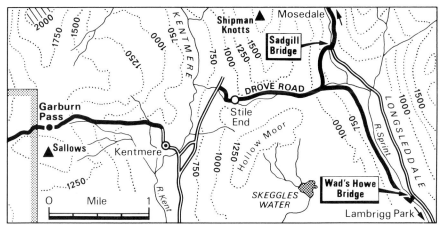

Fig 5.6   Drove Road: Ambleside to Longsleddale

Beyond Sadgill there were two possible routes; one went down the valley, crossing the river at Wad's Howe (496032) and then to Selside and Grayrigg, joining the main drove route at Lambrigg Park. This was evidently a major route, for Wad's Howe Bridge is referred to in about 1750 as being 'in the high road from Ambleside to Appleby'.[13] North of Sadgill, cattle were driven up the valley via the rather steep climb of Gatescarth Pass (since used for quarry traffic) and over into Mosedale where they had a choice of routes, down either Swindale or Wet Sleddale to join the main drove roads to Appleby and Yorkshire, or south into Lancashire. This route has also been described as an 'assize road', along which jurors from this part of Westmorland would have travelled to the assizes in Appleby.

5.2 Packhorse Tracks
Before the construction of the turnpike roads, most goods had to be moved around the Lake District by packhorse — indeed it is likely that before 1750 it was impossible to get most wheeled vehicles westwards from Kendal. Celia Fiennes, writing on her tour in 1697, described her journey from Kendal to Bowness in these terms:

six miles thro' narrow lanes . . . here can be noe carriages but very narrow ones like little wheel-barrows . . . they also use horses on which they have a sort of pannyers . . . and the reason is plaine from the narrowness of the lanes . . . abundance of horses I see all about Kendall streetes with their burdens.[14]

Kendal had become, by then, the marketing centre of the local woollen trade and was served by numerous packhorse routes. At the height of the trade over twenty gangs of packhorses worked in and out of Kendal each week; their destinations including Whitehaven, Cockermouth, Ulverston, Hawkshead, Cartmel, Sedbergh, Orton, Appleby, Penrith, Carlisle, Kirkby Lonsdale and Settle, as well as places further afield such as Glasgow, Barnard Castle, York, Leeds, Hull, Wigan, Manchester, Liverpool, Norwich and London. Packhorses were a flexible and reliable means of transport, but very slow; the journey to London took over two weeks, averaging perhaps only 15 miles a day. Along the packhorse routes trains of up to thirty horses, each carrying loads of up to 3cwt would move in single file. They went from one village to the next, along routes which had been in use since early medieval times, and which in most cases, are still used as roads today. Thus, the vast majority of these routes have been overlain by more modern roads. Occasionally, though, some feature of the old packhorse track remains, as, for example, at Strawberry Bank (413895) and at Underbarrow (475919) on the Kendal to Kirkby Ireleth turnpike, where the zig-zags of the old track survive as the modern road ascends these steep inclines. The modern tourist map still shows sixteen steep hill signs between Kendal and Newby Bridge, though the worst hill, at Strawberry Bank, has a pub half way up!

As with drovers' roads, some pub names connected with packhorses still survive, and can help to give some clues about these old routes. These names include the Pack Horse (Keswick, Seaton and Whitehaven), String of Horses (Faugh, 508550 and Goose Green, near Rosley; 343428) and of course, the Woolpack (Boot, Kendal, Keswick and Penrith).

Sometimes, though, the modern road takes a different route — such as between Lindale (418804) and Haverthwaite. Here the 1818 turnpike, now the A590, takes a longer route via Newby Bridge in order to travel alongside the River Leven through Backbarrow gorge, thus avoiding the hilly ground of the Cartmel peninsula. The packhorse drivers, however, were more likely to have taken a shorter, more direct, route, even if it involved some steep sections, and they no doubt travelled via Broughton (382813) and over the top at Bigland.

Occasionally an article does make an attempt to look at the network of packhorse roads in one particular area, but the evidence is usually scanty, and thus such attempts have been rare. Mary Fair wrote about the routes converging on Eskdale Green:

The road from Broughton came up somewhere near the 'King George' hotel joining that from Ravenglass which turns up to climb the ascent at Randle How just before Eskdale Green station is reached. Beyond the smithy another road came across the bog from an ancient track passing across towards Whitehaven from Muncaster Head direction. There is still a right of way across this soft ground. The road passed through Eskdale Green and up Smithy Brow (where there was another shoeing-forge, now vanished) past Low Holme and through Porterthwaite Wood to Strands and Whitehaven. From this road another branched off up Mitredale, passing over Tongue Moor to Wasdale Head and Cockermouth and Keswick. This road over Tongue Moor was known as 'The Highway'.

Another road passed eastwards up Eskdale on the line of the Roman road over Hardknott Pass, and so to Ambleside, etc. There was also a road under the north side of Muncaster Fell, following the course of the narrow gauge railway track in places; in others it may be seen (notably near Murthwaite) adjoining the line.

Near Eskdale Green railway station there was a tavern on the packhorse route, now marked by a barn. The sign of this tavern hung in a tree. Probably it, like John Nicholson's smithy above it, did an excellent trade when the commerce of the country-side was carried on by the trains of packhorses.[15]

In general, packhorse routes were not engineered or metalled — except where there was some special difficulty, such as boggy ground or steep slopes. In such places, the surface might have been set with large stones in order to maintain the track in a useable condition. As we shall see, such remains can still be found in the mountain passes, especially on the zig-zags which are such a common feature of their steeper sections.

One aspect of the packhorse trade has, however, received more attention, and that is the packhorse bridge.[16] It was one thing to drive cattle or sheep across streams and rivers, but quite another to attempt the same with heavily laden packhorses. Thus, at difficult crossings, packhorse bridges were built, easily recognizable with their typical narrow width and low parapets (Fig 5.7). Very often they now seem to lead nowhere in particular, as the routes which they once served have gone out of use. This is evidently true of Park Bridge near Thornthwaite Hall (515161), where a packhorse route once led from Shap Abbey to its grange at Thornthwaite[17]. Another whose *raison d'être* is no longer obvious is Slater's Bridge in Little Langdale (312030), perhaps built to serve the nearby slate quarries. Other such bridges worth a visit include Monk's Bridge near High Wath on the River Calder (064103), Throstle Garth Bridge on the path from Brotherilkeld into Upper Eskdale (227036), Watendlath Bridge at the end of the road over the much

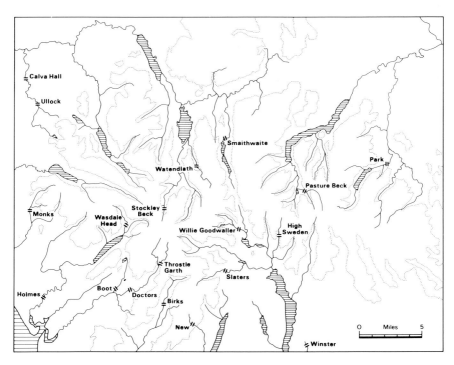

Fig 5.7   Pack Horse Bridges

more recent and well known Ashness Bridge (275164), Doctor's Bridge near the Woolpack Inn in Eskdale — once again widened, but in excellent condition (189008), and Birks Bridge in Dunnerdale (234994). Most of the surviving packhorse bridges seem to have been built between 1660 and 1760, but only one has been dated precisely. In some cases they no doubt replaced earlier bridges, but it is hard to resist the conclusion that the period of their construction coincided with a great growth in trade throughout the Lake District.

The full history of all the Lakeland bridges has yet to be written; J.F. Curwen summed up the situation in North Westmorland in these terms: 'Apart from the great monastic bridges erected by skilled labour sent out from the abbeys, there can be little doubt but that all our early bridges were ... formed of wooden planks resting on cross pieces and supported on stocks or logs.' Stone piers slowly replaced the stocks, and stone arches first appeared in the mid-seventeenth century. 'Afterward, however, narrow stone bridges fit for packhorse traffic multiplied rapidly and they answered their purpose for some hundred years.'[18] Just who paid for the building of packhorse bridges is not at all clear.

Packhorse tracks thus once criss-crossed the whole of the Lake District. In most cases they have been improved and made into metalled roads, though some have gone out of use and remain only as footpaths, if at all. We can only trace these tracks if they are referred to in some contemporary document such as a will, merchant's records or a topographical description. These tracks are rarely used by packhorses now, but an interesting account of a recent journey undertaken by Robert Orrell and two packhorses entitled *Saddle Tramp in the Lake District* is well worth reading.[19] He used several of the mountain passes and some of the lower level packhorse tracks which have avoided being surfaced with tarmac or otherwise improved. These include a route along the southern shore of Ullswater from

Slater's Bridge, Little Langdale

112

Patterdale around to Howtown, and the rather boggy route from Ennerdale to Buttermere via Floutern Tarn. At the end of the Garburn Pass, Orrell comments that Benjamin Browne of Troutbeck, the local magistrate, ordered the pass to be repaired in 1730 because 'it is so utterly much out of repair and in decay that a great part of it is not passable for neither man nor horse to travel through the said ways without danger of being bogged in the moss or lamed among the stones'. His experiences with equally bad routes today prompt him to ask why present day authorities do little or nothing to maintain these 'deteriorating historical routes, ... their consciences are seldom stirred beyond the state of the tarmac ribbon accessible to the motor car'.[20] A more dispassionate observer might well wish that local councils should not even attempt to 'improve' these routes, for there is a very thin line between improvement and destruction.

In order to give the best possible idea of what these tracks were like, the next section of this chapter is devoted to descriptions of the packhorse tracks which still remain intact, namely the mountain passes which have not been made into motor roads.

5.3 Lakeland Passes

The passes have always been important routeways ever since people needed to travel from one valley to the next, for the distance around the mountains was usually very long indeed. We have already seen how the Roman roads over Hard Knott, Wrynose and Whinlatter Passes became drove roads (also used by packhorses), and the corpse roads mentioned in chapter 3 also climb over the lower fells. The major passes of the central Lakeland fells on which remains of the packhorse tracks can still be seen will be described, from Black Sail and Sty Head in the west across to Nan Bield and Gatescarth in the east (Fig 5.8). These routes, which include nine of the ten highest passes in the Lakes, can provide an

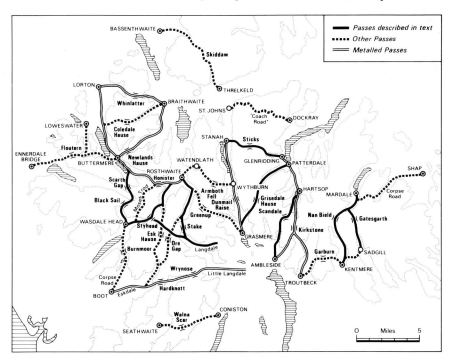

Fig 5.8 Lakeland Passes

interesting alternative to an ascent of the higher fells, perhaps when the weather is less than perfect; there is nothing worse than struggling up to a summit and being able to see absolutely nothing. These passes are the original tracks across the fells, dating from the days before fell-walking. Only three of them rise to over 2,000ft, and yet all are higher than the Kirkstone, the highest metalled pass. An enjoyable and sometimes strenuous day's walking can be had by stringing together two or three passes to make a circular route if necessary. Travelling over these routes will give a very clear notion of the difficulties facing the packhorse men (and the packhorses!) in the days before the modern road system was completed. Only one book has ever been written specifically about Lakeland passes — and although long out of print, it is often to be found in secondhand bookshops, and makes excellent light reading, as does a chapter in one of William Palmer's books, describing cycling over four unmade passes early this century.[21] Today's walker is advised to take the Ordnance Survey 1:25,000 scale Outdoor Leisure maps.

Scarth Gap and Black Sail   This route is best tackled from Buttermere; the path leaves from Gatescarth Farm (194150) and after crossing the head of Buttermere makes a very easy ascent of the pass, until the 1,200ft contour where the original zig-zags have been cut by modern fell-walkers (Fig 5.9). At the summit (1,400ft) Great Gable, Kirk Fell and Pillar come into view almost simultaneously giving what the Ward Lock guide book for 1918 called 'The sternest and grandest "surprise" view in the district.' The descent to the youth hostel at the head of Ennerdale is gentle, but the ascent of Black Sail is steeper and rougher. Again there are some zig-zags on both sides of the summit, notably just before the crossing of Gatherstone Beck where there used to be a bridge (184108). The path now keeps to the north-east side of Mosedale Beck down to Wasdale Head, but at some time the path may have forded the beck (at184096) and continued down the opposite bank to the packhorse bridge (187088), which otherwise would have led to nowhere in particular.

Sty Head   When Thomas Gray visited Borrowdale in 1769 he was told the absurd story that Sty Head was only passable for a few weeks each year — no doubt the locals did not want strangers wandering around the hills, for smuggling was a very profitable trade in these parts until William Pitt the Younger reduced the duties towards the end of the century; contraband came in via Ireland and the Isle of Man, and the remote Cumberland coast was ideally suited to receive it.

Sty Head was always the best used pass between Borrowdale and the south, and its importance can be gauged from the fact that it was engineered for almost all its length. Hutchinson's *History of Cumberland* (1794) says that a road from Egremont to Keswick was 'forming through the village' of Wasdale Head, and at the end of the last century there was a scheme to put a 'coach road' over it.

In 1896 the self-taught County Surveyor, George Bell, actually surveyed a route, which, if it had ever been built, would have been one of the most curious in Britain. From Wasdale Head he proposed to take the road around the head of Mosedale at a gradient not exceeding 1 in 12, and generally only 1 in 20, thus reaching over 1,000ft before it even turned towards Sty Head (Fig 5.10). It was then to slant gently across the face of Kirk Fell and Great Gable to reach the top of the pass, but having taken four miles instead of the two miles of the direct route. Its descent into Borrowdale was to be almost as gentle, this time curving south into Grains Gill, and crossing the stream half a mile above Stockley Bridge.

Baddeley's *Guide* of 1902 noted the projected road, but said that the scheme was still *'in nubilius'* (ie in the clouds, in more ways than one!). Barber and Atkinson, writing in 1927 were in no doubt about the propriety of such schemes: 'Spasmodic attempts — hitherto, fortunately, unsuccessful — are made to re-open the question of making roads over Wrynose and Hard Knott and Sty Head, but when

114

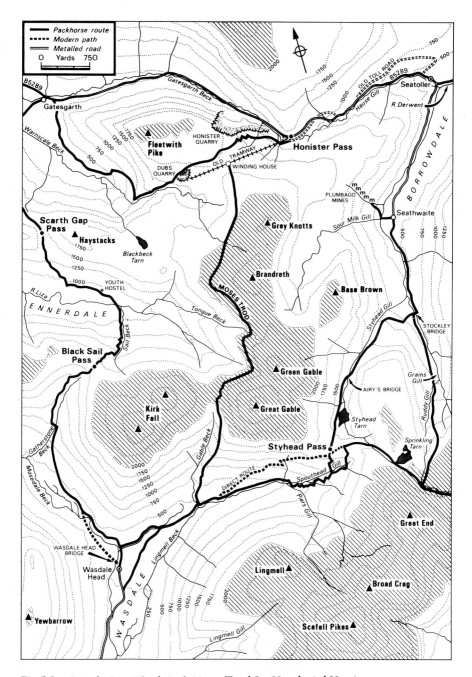

Fig 5.9   Scarth Gap, Black Sail, Moses Trod Sty Head and Honister

the road-maker with his tar engines and steam rollers invades the privacy of these passes their attractiveness will at once disappear. To drive roads through them would be an act of sheer vandalism. . . .' Two of these passes have succumbed but Sty Head remains untouched by the grinding queues of cars which now thread their laborious way over Hard Knott and Wrynose. Indeed, Sty Head was still being maintained as a packhorse route as late as 1930.[22]

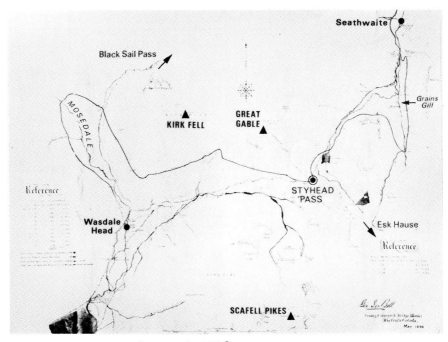

Fig 5.10   Sty Head Road proposals, 1896

Zig-zags on the Sty Head Pass

The summit of Sty Head Pass

Stockley Bridge

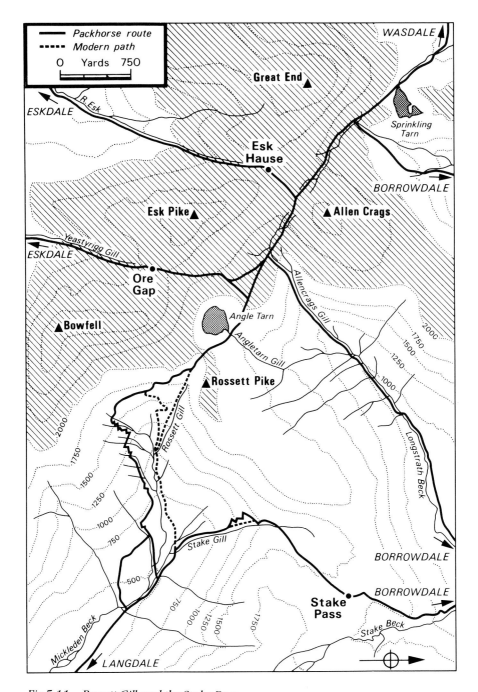

Fig 5.11   Rossett Gill and the Stake Pass

The name Sty (or Stee) means a 'ladder', and this could well refer to the zig-zags on the original path. The modern hiker habitually takes the very rough and stony route across the lower slopes of Great Gable, but the old route is much more gently graded, and still has grass underfoot for most of the way. It may take five or ten minutes longer to ascend the pass this way, but it is time well spent. The point where the valley path diverges from the direct 'tourist' route is about ¼ mile beyond the Gable Beck footbridge (202093); it crosses Spouthead Gill at 212092 (marked by cairns, but easily missed), and back again at 218092; leading from there fairly directly to the summit of the pass (the OS map is wrong and Wainwright right: see Fig 5.9 [23]). Beyond the summit, which is at little more than 1,600ft, the route drops down by Sty Head Tarn, crosses Styhead Gill at Airy's Bridge (224104) and after a gentle half mile with several sections of the old road still intact, it drops more steeply down into Borrowdale; much of the old causey of this descent has recently been rebuilt. Stockley Bridge is another packhorse bridge, said to have been widened in 1887, but still quite narrow, even though rebuilt after the floods of 1966. The path down to Seathwaite used to be well made and metalled, but the combination of hikers and floods has destroyed most of the old way.

From Stockley Bridge another pass leads south into the hills, ascending Grains Gill and Ruddy Gill to Esk Hause, and then dropping into Eskdale, though the first habitation (Brotherilkeld Farm) is still five miles distant from the summit. This is always listed as the highest of the Lakeland passes at 2,490ft, but it is doubtful whether it was ever much used — there is little in the way of a path south of the summit. Much the same also applies to Ore Gap, a little further to the east, although, as we have already seen, the monks of Furness Abbey must have used one or other of these passes to link their estates in Borrowdale and Eskdale.

Stake Pass and Rossett Gill From the head of Langdale, two passes lead on into the fells. To the north is the Stake Pass, leading over to Langstrath and Borrowdale — a well engineered route with a whole set of zig-zags and some paving as it ascends the hill alongside Stake Gill (Fig 5.11). As usual, the modern tourist habitually ignores the twists and turns of the old track, preferring a route straight up or down the slope. The zig-zags have thus been preserved, and they provide a route which is easier (both in ascent and descent), almost as quick, and certainly much more interesting than the new route. The path crosses the gill at 260082 and winds its way across the curious topography of Langdale Combe (the result of the very last minor glaciation) before reaching its modest summit of 1,576ft, and dropping, via more zig-zags into Langstrath.

Back at the head of Langdale, the pass straight ahead is Rossett Gill — certainly the most infamous ascent in the whole of the Lake District; every year thousands of hikers clamber up and down the stony bed of the gill, many unaware of the two zig-zags to the south, and almost all totally unaware of the old pony track which takes an entirely different route. Its starting point in Langdale is now difficult to see, and the path is much more easily found from the top of the pass — where it coincides with the upper zig-zag for a short distance. It keeps to the slopes of Bowfell, and avoids the gill altogether, eventually joining the present day path some 500yd below the junction of the Stake Pass and Rossett Gill routes.[24]

Once the Gill has been ascended, the path drops a hundred feet or so to Angle Tarn, and then climbs once again. This route does not pass the true summit of Esk Hause, but by-passes it to the north a hundred feet lower down, and then descends to Sprinkling Tarn and the top of Sty Head Pass.

Sticks Pass This pass links Thirlmere and Keswick on the one side with Ullswater on the other, and was no doubt first used intensively when mining became important in Elizabethan times. The pass is the highest ever in general use (2,420ft) and yet its ascent is remarkably easy. Starting from the Thirlmere side at Stanah (318189) a fine set of zig-zags ascends Stanah Gill, levelling out at about 1,600ft into a gently rising path which crosses the flanks of Stybarrow Dodd towards Sticks Gill and the summit. The route was once marked by a series of sticks (hence its name); these have long since disappeared, but the route is still well cairned. The descent starts equally gently into a large basin-shaped area once more deeply ponded to provide a head of water to power the lead mine and smelt works below. Beyond Stang End (362178) the path drops steeply down zig-zags, which have been improved at one time to take wheeled vehicles, to the old Glenridding lead mine, and then down the well-graded road to Ullswater.

If the Sticks Pass was impassable because of snow or mist, then another road crossed these hills, only three miles further north, and still incorrectly marked on

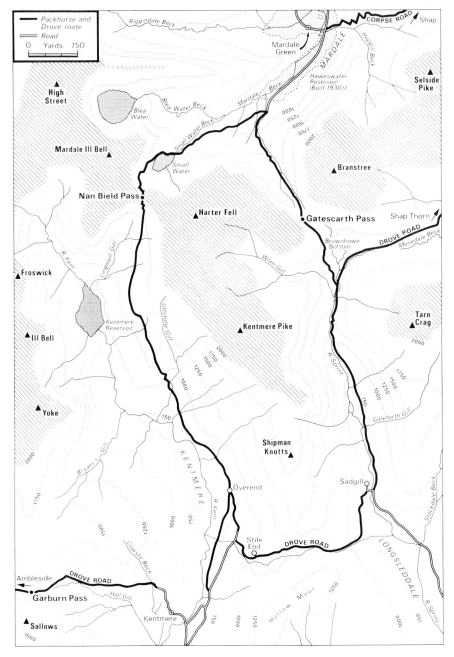

Fig 5.12   Nan Bield and Gatescarth

The old road across Threlkeld Common

Ordnance maps as an 'old coach road'. It leads from Wanthwaite in St John's in the Vale across Threlkeld Common to Dockray, Matterdale and Ullswater. There is no evidence that it was ever used regularly by coaches — for they usually went round by Scales and Troutbeck — its most likely origins are as a peat-road and for general cart traffic. The road was evidently well made, and the ascent at the western end is remarkably even and could be tackled without difficulty by a four-wheel drive vehicle even now. It reaches its summit of 1,434ft after two miles, and then follows the contours for a further three miles to High Row, above Dockray. It might be regarded as heresy to say so, but this is a route which could easily be surfaced, and which would open up a neglected corner of the Lakes, without causing any serious damage to the landscape; the views from this road are certainly spectacular.

Grisedale Hause   This route, linking Grasmere and Ullswater, is still marked on Ordnance Survey maps as an 'Old Packhorse Road'. It is best seen starting from the southern end, at Mill Bridge (336092). After barely half a mile the track divides — the main route keeps left up Little Tongue, but the alternative route, both shorter and easier, ascends Tongue Gill; the two routes meet at 349112, and continue rather roughly to the summit (1,930ft). Just before, though, yet another zig-zag (to the east) avoids the worst of the final climb. The path then drops down to Grisedale Tarn, and follows the valley all the rather long way down to Patterdale. The word *hause,* incidentally, derives from the Norse *hals* meaning a pass or a steep way over.

Scandale Pass   This pass is an alternative route to the Kirkstone pass, but it requires an extra 300ft of ascent, and has never been as much used, especially as the Romans seem to have chosen Kirkstone. Nevertheless, it makes an excellent walk from Ambleside. The route starts a little above the town from the Kirkstone road (at 377047) along Sweden Bridge Lane. Keeping to the right after 100yd, the narrow lane leads through delightful country to the fine packhorse bridge at High Sweden Bridge (379068) and then along Scandale Bottom for a mile and a half before the climb to the summit begins. Beyond, the path follows Caiston Beck, joining what may have been the Roman road at about 399109. If a round trip back

The quarry road up Gatescarth Pass

to Ambleside is needed, then an interesting route is to leave the pass at its summit and make the ascent of Red Screes. From here, the ridge back to Ambleside can be followed, the walls narrowing down to become an enclosed lane (387070) which leads on down the ridge, joining the Kirkstone Pass route less than a mile above Ambleside.

Nan Bield and Gatescarth   In recent times the eastern fells of Lakeland have been quiet and peaceful, even at Bank Holidays, but it was not always so, for the valleys of Kentmere and Longsleddale both provided routes over into Mardale, thus linking Kendal and Penrith. However, the route over Shap became the preferred route, and these two passes further west have remained unimproved (Fig 5.12).

The Nan Bield Pass starts from Kentmere village, but on the opposite side of the river, going first to Overend (484057), and starting the remarkably gentle ascent about a mile further on. It takes almost two miles to climb 1,000ft, and it is not until the summit is almost reached that the path becomes steep, and sharp zig-zags tackle the final 300ft of ascent to a height of 2,100ft. Almost immediately, the path drops away on the other side, the sharp crest making this undoubtedly the finest of all the Lakeland passes. The path zig-zags and curves, dropping down to Small Water, where it crosses the beck, and heads for Haweswater. The submerged village of Mardale Green is shown on the map as it was a century ago.

Gatescarth Pass can be used as a return route; it goes around the other side of Harter Fell, and again has some zig-zags on the ascent, which have been negotiated by a coach-and-four. Beyond the summit the road drops gently to Brownhowe Bottom where the drove road from the south led off eastwards towards Shap. However, continuing down the valley, a shock is in store, for the track, now made up as a quarry road, drops very steeply indeed alongside a rocky gorge into Longsleddale; the twentieth-century road-builders had no choice but to keep the main zig-zag of the old packhorse route, though the rest has been straightened out. Just above the zig-zag, there are some stepping stones in the wall, and behind, a short section of the original track can still be seen. A mile and a half down the valley, Sadgill is reached, and the low col back to Kentmere completes the round trip.

Other Passes   There are numerous other unmetalled passes which have been used at various times and which can still be followed by the ingenious walker. They include Coledale Hause across the north-western fells, the long track from Threlkeld to Bassenthwaite across Skiddaw Forest, and the alternative routes between Borrowdale and Grasmere, either by Greenup Edge, or by Watendlath, Armboth Fell and Wythburn. The Walna Scar road between Coniston and Dunnerdale is an excellent route, complete with a widened packhorse bridge at 271966, built to serve the extensive quarries thereabouts.[25] The quarry roads around Honister, however, deserve a short section to themselves.

5.4   Honister and Moses Trod

Slate was first quarried at Honister in 1643 and its extraction has continued ever since. The best slate is found high on the crags, notably around the 2,000ft contour on Fleetwith Pike, and thus getting the slate down to the valleys has always been something of a problem. The pass itself was not used for this purpose until the nineteenth century; before that, slate was taken to the coast to be transported further, and this led to the creation of two routes. The first was called Moses Trod which led over the high fells and down into Wasdale, heading for the coast at Ravenglass or Drigg. The second route became more important in the mid-nineteenth century when Workington and Whitehaven became the main ports. In this case the slate was either carried by packhorses down the track into Warnscale Bottom, or was loaded on to the wooden sleds and these were 'run' down the scree slopes of Fleetwith Pike towards Buttermere, an extremely hazardous undertaking, which continued until about 1880. Finally, the pass itself was improved during the late nineteenth century (including a toll road on the Borrowdale side built by the quarry company) and it became part of the tourists' round trip from Keswick.

An early description of the pass was given in a letter to the *Gentleman's Magazine* in 1749. The writer, one George Smith, had been to see the black lead or graphite mines, and then proceeded to tackle Honister:

we had a mountain to climb for above 700 yards, in a direction so nearly

Honister – the old and new roads

perpendicular that we were in doubt whether we should attempt it . . . the whole mountain is called Unnisterre or, as I suppose, Finisterre, for such it appears to be; . . . in about another hour we gained the summit . . . the scene was terrifying.

. . the horrid projection of vast promontories; the vicinity of the clouds, the
thunder of the explosions in the slate quarries, the dreadful solitude, the
distance of the plain below, and the mountains heaped on mountains that were

The start of the old toll road above Seatoller

piled around us, desolate and waste, like the ruins of a world which we only had survived, excited such ideas of horror as are not to be expressed.

The exploration of these routes is best begun at Seatoller in Borrowdale (Fig 5.9). Immediately above the hamlet, the old toll road leads off on the right-hand side of the road (244138), providing a pleasanter, car-free, though somewhat rough alternative to the present motor road. Half a mile up the toll road another old, but well-made, road leads northwards to Grange. The two roads run independently to the summit, the old toll road remaining above the present road almost until the top. The north side of the pass was never much improved until the middle of this century, and before then guide books hardly encouraged the traveller: 'the descent is at a walking pace, and nervous passengers may remember that the drivers attach considerable value to their own necks.' 'The first part of the descent . . . is very rough and steep, so much so that vehicles, trying to return by it from Buttermere, are liable to come to a dead-lock. The attempt, we believe, is not often made.'[26] To the south-west are the scree slopes of Fleetwith Pike used as sled runs up to a hundred years ago.

Returning to the summit of the pass, the old tramway, which was built to replace sled running, can be ascended as far as the foundations of the winding house (216135). It is from here that one of the most curious routes in the whole of the Lake District leads over the high fells for more than three miles to Wasdale. This is Moses Trod, supposedly named after a famous quarryman who reputedly distilled or stored whisky on this exposed fellside — another part of the smuggling trade. The very idea of transporting slate on sleds over such country may now seem odd, if not ludicrous, but a glance at the map will show that this route takes a remarkably

126

The north side of Honister Pass

direct line to the nearest point on the coast, some 14 miles away; the later alternative routes, to Whitehaven or Workington, were half as long again and poorly served with roads. The track has been popularised by Wainwright, though Molly Lefebure suggests that the 'real' Moses Trod lies 200ft lower down the fell-side.[27]

The track starts from the old winding house and climbs Grey Knotts before contouring around Brandreth and Green Gable. It then goes into Stone Cove at the very head of Ennerdale and across to Beck Head between Great Gable and Kirk Fell. From here it first slants across and then goes directly down the steep south-western rib of Great Gable to reach the valley floor about a mile and a half from the lake. Slate may then have been sent down Wastwater by boat, and on by packhorse or cart to the coast. The fell part of the route is often referred to as a sledgate (ie a way for sleds), but whether sleds loaded with the slate could have negotiated the whole of this route is difficult to say. At least the contraband whisky and rum could be carried on horseback.

Generally packhorses were used for transporting slate and other minerals; one only has to see how many bridleways in the Lakes lead up to quarries. All the slate quarries had special routes; those around Coniston used the lake for transport, and the slate was then taken overland to Greenodd. Slate from the Burlington quarries (250840) was usually exported through Sandside on the Duddon estuary, but after the Ulverton canal opened in 1796, a specially constructed 'slate road' was built, via Cocklakes and Netherhouses, even though this involved a journey over twice as long.[28]

5.5 Mining and Industrial Routes

The first large-scale industry to arrive in the Lake District came in the rather unlikely form of fifty or so German miners and smelters who were brought to Keswick in the 1560s. The deposits of copper and also of lead had been known for many years, but the setting up of the Society of the Mines Royal by a charter of Elizabeth I in 1564 was to increase output; it also increased both local population and trade. We know much about the operations of the company, for many of its account books have survived, and they often give day to day details, including some indication of the roads then in use.[29] Wood, charcoal and peat were brought in from an ever widening area, and even some coal was brought from the coast. It is interesting to note that stone coal cost $\frac{3}{4}$d a horse load, but it then cost 9d to transport it from Cockermouth to Keswick, and a further 1d to the smelter at Brigham, a mile further east. To put this into perspective, the daily wage for a smelter was 6d, which would also buy thirty 'big nails'. Again, it cost 6s 0d to transport four casks of wine from Newcastle (via the Tyne and Eden valleys and Penrith). These costs illustrate graphically the difficulties of transport in the north of England at this time. Nevertheless, facilities for transport, although expensive, were better than one might have expected. The use of Newcastle as the main port is a little surprising, but it was evidently preferred to the undeveloped alternative of Workington, even for the export of the heavy finished ingots.

Longer journeys are also recorded in the accounts; George Needham travelled up from London in 1568, and after reaching Lancaster, travelled around the Lakes in search of supplies of wood and charcoal:

Guide over Sands to Mr. Christopher Preston [Holker], 2s., to Mr. P.'s man 6d. Guide over (Leven) Sands to Mr. John Preston [Furness Abbey], 1s. 4d. To Mr. J.P.'s man after staying 2 days and 2 nights, 2s. Sending letter to the Queen's Beli [bailiff] in Fornesfels, 1s.4d. At Colton Chapel, dinner with C. Preston, Mr. Braddyll and 13 men, to swear they would act according to the Commission in regard to the Queen's woods, 13s 4d. To Gresmor [Grasmere] with Mr. B. the night, 4s. Letter to the Queen's bailiff in Barnthal [Borrowdale], 1s. Borrowdale, food and drink, 2s.4d. Another dinner there with Mr. B. and the sworn men 12s. .

. . . Keswick to Rebenglas [Ravenglass] and by the seashore to inspect the harbour and Mr. Corbins [Curwen's] ground, 10s. 7d. Guide, 3s. 4d. To Carlin

[Carlisle] to Milordt Bischoff [the Bishop] on business about the woods, 5s. 8d. With H. Reinbrun three times to Kaugart [Calgarth, Mr. Philipson's] to buy wood, 8s. 4d. With H. Reinbrun to Kirkuswald to see the Duke of Norfolk, 2 days and nights, 12s. 8d. Twice to Workington, 4s. 9d. With H. Reinbrun to Borrowdale, to see about charcoal, 2s. and to Mr. Porter's, 1s. In all £10.4.3.[30]

In the accounts for 1571 there are lists of the numerous local people involved in the carriage of goods; peat was being brought from Skiddaw and from near the old Roman forts at Troutbeck, along a packhorse route via Brundholme (289250). Charcoal was being produced all around the edge of Borrowdale and the Newlands Valley, and was even being brought over Dunmail Raise from High Furness. Of course the ore itself was arriving from Coniston, Caldbeck, Borrowdale, and especially from the Newlands Valley which had the richest mine known as God's Gift (Gotes Gab — eventually known locally as Goldscope) (231184). Derwentwater was used for transport (there are accounts for the building of boats) and Keswick Bridge was rebuilt. Certainly the choice of Keswick as the focal point for this enterprise was a shrewd one. Unfortunately, the company collapsed in 1579, but various individuals kept it going on a smaller scale until the Civil War.

Another mineral also attracted much attention in this area — namely graphite, also known as wadd, plumbago or black lead, found near Seathwaite. It was first discovered in 1555 and was used in glazing pottery, casting cannon balls, preventing rust, as a medicinal cure, and finally in 1792, in pencils. The mines were thought so important by 1752 that an Act of Parliament was passed to ensure their protection, and they formed part of the usual tour of Borrowdale by the end of that century. Apart from a short stretch of cobbled road leading from the mines, the plumbago gave rise to no special roads — it was simply carried along the main road through Borrowdale to Keswick, and several maps appeared in the eighteenth century depicting this route (Fig 4.13).

The rapid growth of various types of industry must have led to the use of certain routes by one particular trade, whether it was the iron ore carried to High Furness to be smelted in medieval times, or the vast array of later industries from bobbins to gunpowder. One rather curious industry has specific routes associated with it, and that is the manufacture of snuff, which became important in the eighteenth century. The tobacco was imported at Whitehaven, and two 'snuff pack roads' have been identified.[31] The first led to Ennerdale, then via Floutern Tarn to Buttermere, Newlands, and Keswick to the mills at Penrith. The second went further south through Egremont and Gosforth, over the Hard Knott and Wrynose Passes to Ambleside and the centre of the industry at Kendal. There were also mills further east at Newbiggin and Kirkby Stephen. The identification of such routes comes in rather the same category as the 'saltways' mentioned in chapter 3, for these routes were never used solely for transporting snuff or rather the raw tobacco used in the process. It is likely that these routes were more widely used for the movement of supplies of illicit spirits from remote western Lakeland to the towns further south and east!

5.6 Over-the-Sands

Before the reorganisation of the county boundaries in 1974, the peninsulas of Furness and Cartmel were usually referred to as 'Lancashire-North-of-the-Sands', and indeed until the middle of the last century, the usual route from Lancaster to this detached section of the county lay across the sands of Morecambe Bay. This route was always preferred for the good and simple reason that it was far shorter than going 'over-land'. In the village of Cartmel a milestone gives the over-sands

Milestone at Cartmel

LANCASTER
OVER SANDS **15** MILES
ULVERSTON
OVER SANDS **7** MILES

GRANGE

CARK

distance to Lancaster as only 15 miles. The distance to Lancaster on the old packhorse route via Kendal is 36 miles, and even the later turnpike (A590 and A6) via Levens Bridge is 25 miles. The long way round to Ulverston is 11 miles, and although this is not much longer than the sands route (7 miles), the latter had the advantage of an easy run for wheeled traffic for a third of the distance, and virtually no hills en route. Of course, the sands routes had their disadvantages — they could only be used when the tide was out, and they could easily be dangerous if the route was lost (perhaps in mist), if the safe passage across the river channels had changed, or if travellers were caught by quicksands, by the incoming tide, or drowned in deep holes made by boats unloading at the previous low tide. Nevertheless, it is a measure of the importance of these routes that stage coaches continued to use them for many years after the coastal turnpike road was opened.

The early history of the sands crossings is difficult to trace; we have already seen that one medieval clerk thought that Furness Abbey was situated on an island — and so it might have been as far as the rest of England was concerned. The first record of the crossing appears in 1322 when Robert the Bruce invaded and plundered much of Cumbria. He rode down the west coast from Holm Cultram to Furness where the abbot paid him a ransom. The Lanercost Chronicle continues the story:

> Also they went further beyond the sands of Leven to Cartmell, and burnt the lands round the Priory of the Black Canons, taking away cattle and spoil. And so they crossed the sands of Kent, as far as the town of Lancaster, which they burnt.[32]

Four years later the Abbot of Furness petitioned Edward II for the appointment of a coroner in Furness because 'in the crossing over the sands between the parts of Furness and the town of Lancaster at the ebb of the sea, many men ... in making the crossing ... oft in past times have stood in danger'.[33] In effect, people travelling to attend the coroner's court in Lancaster had been drowned on the journey!

The three local monasteries of Furness, Conishead and Cartmel probably appointed the first guides over the sands, although there is no actual record of any of them until the 1530s, just before the dissolution of the monasteries. Cartmel Priory, for example, paid for a 'bailiff and conductor of all the King's people over the sands of the sea' in 1535, and the post was so vital that it was kept on by the Duchy of Lancaster after the dissolution. Curiously, the sixteenth-century guides over the Kent Sands either had or took the name of Carter, and the guides have been known by that name ever since. It seems quite likely that the early guides were in fact carters who had a vital need to know the safe routes across the shifting channels.[34]

The difficulties of the crossing have often been over-stated, but they did, on occasions, lead to loss of life — usually one or two deaths each year. The registers of Cartmel Priory Church alone record 141 people drowned on the sands in the three hundred years up to 1880. Local papers record more detail of accidents in the nineteenth century, with various causes such as 'drowned', 'got into quicksand', 'overtaken by the tide', 'surrounded by the tide', 'fell into deep water', 'coach blown over', and 'cart upset in Black Scars Hole'.[35] In 1820 there was even a plan to erect platforms above the high water mark as refuges, but it seems that only one was ever built.

Despite the difficulties, a public convenyance began a regular service across the sands from Lancaster to Ulverston in 1781. The owners claimed that they had 'procured a sober and careful driver who is well acquainted with the sands, and humbly hope that their plan will meet with due encouragement as this is the most cheap, safe and expeditious method of crossing the sands to and from Ulverston'.[35] Public services across the sands continued despite the opening of the new turnpike via Levens Bridge in 1820, for the new road was still much longer and tolls had to be paid. In fact the sands route remained in common use until the coastal railway line was completed in 1857 which, although again still longer than the sands route, was much quicker, and could be undertaken at any state of the tide! Coaches, it must be remembered, had to leave when the tide was on the ebb; in September 1848 daily departure times varied between 7.20am and 4pm! The mileages of the various routes between Lancaster and Ulverston can be summarised thus:

Old Packhorse Route — 1763 Turnpike via Kendal	41 miles
1818 Turnpike via Levens Bridge	35 miles
1857 Railway	25 miles
Over the sands	19 miles

The route did not end at Ulverton, but continued across the Furness peninsula to Ireleth where the Duddon sands could be crossed to Millom, and then on up the coast to the crossing of the Esk just before Ravenglass. The whole route was traversed by John Wesley in 1759; and described in his *Journal:*

Sat 12 [May] Setting out early [from Flookborough], we came to Bottle [Bootle], about twenty-four measured miles from Fluckborough, soon after eight, having crossed the Millam Sand [Millom — ie the Duddon Sands], without either guide or difficulty. Here we were informed that we could not pass at Ravenglass before one or two o'clock; whereas, had we gone on, as we afterwards found, we might have passed immediately. About eleven we were directed to a Ford, near Manchester Hall [Muncaster], which they said we might cross at noon. When we came thither, they told us we could not cross; so we sat still till about one. We then found we could have crossed at noon. However, we reached Whitehaven before night. But I have taken my leave of the sand road. I believe it is ten measured miles shorter than the other [ie overland, by Kendal and Dunmail Raise]: but there are four sands to pass, so far from each other, that it is scarce possible to pass them all in a day: Especially as you have all the way to do with a generation of liars, who detain all strangers as long as they can, either for their own gain or their neighbours'. I can advise no stranger to go this way: He may go round by Kendal and Keswick, often in less time, always with less expense, and far less trial of his patience.[37]

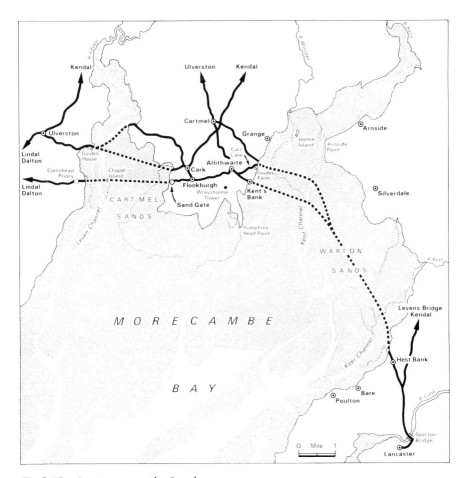

Fig 5.13   Routes across the Sands

Not all travellers found the route so arduous; Thomas West in his *Guide* of 1780 assured his readers that 'with the proper guides, crossing of the sands in summer is thought a journey of little more danger than any other. . . . On a fine day there is not a more pleasant sea-side journey in the Kingdom.' The editor of this second edition of the *Guide* did however feel it necessary to add a few words to West's own description of the distant views, for he hardly mentions the sands crossing at all:

[West's] description of this curious and pleasing ride is, as far as it goes, just, but not characteristic. What most attracts the notice of the traveller is not the objects of the surrounding country but *the sands themselves*. . . . As he pursues his *often-trackless* way he will recollect, that probably but a few hours before, the whole expanse was covered with some fathoms of water, and that in a few more it will as certainly be covered again. At the same time he may also perceive, on his left hand, the retreated ocean ready to obey the mysterious laws of its irresistible movement, without any visible barrier to stay it a moment where it is. . . . But when the traveller reaches the side of the *Eau* [ie the channel of the River Kent], these affections will be greatly increased. He there drops down a gentle descent to the edge of a broad and seemingly impassable river, where the only remains he can perceive of the surrounding lands are the tops of distant mountains, and where a solitary being on horseback (like some antient genius of the deep) is deseried hovering on its brink, or encountering its stream with gentle steps, in order to conduct him through it. When fairly entered into the water, if a stranger to this scene, and he do not feel himself touched with some of the most pleasing emotions, I should think him destitute of common sensibility. For, in the midst of apparently great danger, he will soon find that there is really none at all.[38]

This route was certainly regarded as safe, and almost an essential part of the tour of the Lakes. Since then the literature of the sands crossing has grown enormously — so many writers have recorded their own and other peoples' experiences and impressions; apart from those already quoted, a brief list might include George Fox, Robert Southey, Ann Radcliffe, Thomas De Quincey, William Wordsworth, Harriet Martineau, and Mrs Gaskell, right through to Jessica Lofthouse, and one of the present guides, Cedric Robinson.[39]

The route taken by the coaches can still be followed throughout, but the crossings of the channels of the main rivers can be treacherous, and should not be attempted without the guide. Several times each year guided parties, usually numbering several hundred people, are taken across — details are advertised locally. Anyone venturing on the sands should contact the guides: the Kent guide lives at Guide's Farm, Cart Lane, Grange-over-Sands (Tel: 2165) and the Leven guide at Levens House, Canal Foot, Ulverston (Tel: 54156).

In the old days the coaches set out from Lancaster, either from the King's Arms or the Bear and Staff, and crossed the Lune at Skerton Bridge (rebuilt in 1788) then heading north to Hest Bank. The coaches timed their departure so that they would set out across the sands between four and eight hours after high tide. The Hest Bank Hotel had a specially built lantern room and a bright light was lit at dusk to guide travellers coming in the opposite direction. The route across to the Cartmel peninsula never went direct but curved round, keeping a mile or so from the shore as far north as Silverdale (Fig 5.13). The map shows the coastline and channels as

Cart Lane – used by sands traffic after crossing the Kent.

133

The main street of Flookburgh; the old route lay straight ahead, but the main road now turns right where the car is emerging

they were just before the railway was built. After about a mile and a half came the first hazard, the crossing of the channel of the River Keer, and from 1820 until 1860 an assistant guide was appointed specifically to mark this crossing, for the area was noted for its quicksands. Once across the Keer, the coaches usually had a good run over firm sand for four miles or more before having to turn westwards to cross the channel or channels at the River Kent. The Kent is a sizeable river, and its flow can be swift, though it is not usually more than two feet deep at low tide. The changes in the channels from year to year can be seen well from Grange-over-Sands; in the mid-1970s, for example, the main channel of the Kent was very close to the shore, but it has since moved back to its more usual position about half a mile out. On the first Ordnance Survey map, on the other hand, the channel clung to the opposite shore around Arnside Point. Once the coaches had forded the Kent *terra firma* was not far away, and they usually came ashore either at Kents Bank, or near Guide's Farm and Cart Lane (401765). The distance across the Kent Sands was usually about eight miles.

The coaches then climbed to Allithwaite and across to Flookburgh, passing Wraysholme Tower (383754) which until the land reclamation of the 1780s and 1790s, used to stand almost on the shore. This is a fourteenth-century pele tower probably built in the years after Bruce's raid of 1322; in the late eighteenth century it belonged to the Carter family (ie the guides over the sands). Flookburgh may now seem a forgotten place, but it had a borough charter in medieval times, and up to 1860 it was the major stopping place between Lancaster and Ulverston; Grange and Kent's Bank were then little more than hamlets. It had inns and lodging houses for travellers who had missed the tides, and its half-mile long main street attests to the importance of the sands traffic. Now, the western end of this street (still called Main Street) leads nowhere, and traffic turns north in the middle of the town. The original route continued directly westwards onto the sands again at Sand Gate (354757), but early in the nineteenth century coaches began to go north from Flookborough to Cark, avoiding the hill at Sand Gate, and gaining easier access to the sands.

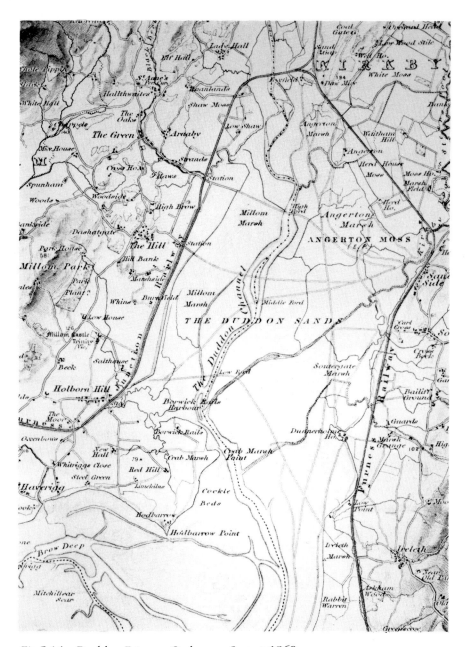

Fig 5.14   *Duddon Estuary: Ordnance Survey, 1869*

The crossing of the Leven Sands, though only three miles in length, often caused more problems than the much longer crossing of the Kent estuary. 'You mun nivver stand still on t'sands', guides used to warn travellers in carriages, 't'sand'll be washed from under t'wheels by t'current and afore ye know wheer y'are ye'll have topplet over. And ye may verra wheel be ower t'heads in t'watter.'[40] Just over half way across, though well to the south of the usual route, lies Chapel Island, which probably acted as a refuge in medieval times when the route lay further south, heading for Conishead Priory and ultimately Furness Abbey. In fact, the island is

Chapel Island in the Leven estuary

almost opposite Conishead Priory, but it is not mentioned until 1593 when it was called Harlsyde, and it was not referred to as Chapel Island until 1736. The present ruins were erected on top of earlier ruins as a folly for the new Gothic mansion of Conishead Priory built in the 1820s. At present, the island can be reached dry-shod from the Cartmel shore, because the channel of the Leven lies to the west of the island. However, the channel occasionally shifts to the east side of the island; Pape noted this in 1934, and the present author saw the same occurrence in the late 1970s. The main coach route came ashore at the point which is now the mouth of the Ulverston Canal (314776), only a mile and a half from Ulverston.

For travellers going further, the route continued across the Furness peninsula via Lindal to Ireleth (223776) before crossing the River Duddon to Holborn Hill (now Millom). The first edition Ordnance Survey map shows a plethora of routes across the Duddon estuary, specifically naming the High, Middle, and Low Fords across the channel (Fig 5.14). It is worth remembering that in 1850 the industrial towns of Millom, Askam and, above all, Barrow, did not exist, and thus no roads were needed to serve them. Going further up the coast, early travellers had only the three river crossings near Ravenglass to face, though as we have already seen, crossing the Esk was difficult enough to upset John Wesley.

Turnpikes

6.1 The Need For New Roads

The previous two chapters have attempted to show that, from Elizabethan times onwards, there was an ever increasing need for adequate roads for the movement of both people and goods. Moreover, the population of the area had been growing rapidly (almost doubling during the eighteenth century) so that at the first Census in 1801, Cumberland, Westmorland, Furness and Cartmel had some 176,000 inhabitants. The towns were growing more rapidly than the countryside, and this was chiefly due to increased industrial production and the general growth in trade.

Along the western coast the coal and iron ore fields were being exploited, and Whitehaven and Workington were growing rapidly as both towns and ports under the control of the Lowther and Senhouse families respectively. By 1801, for example, Whitehaven had 8,700 inhabitants, and Workington 5,700, compared to 6,900 in Kendal and 10,200 in Carlisle which was by then developing a textile industry. The agricultural sector was also growing rapidly, though the various improvements often took over a century to reach Cumbria from southern England. Farming was clearly encouraged by the growth in population, particularly in the towns, and was again aided by a few forward-looking landowners. Many thousands of acres were enclosed, particularly between 1795 and 1830, improving productivity and entirely changing the landscape. The new roads created by enclosure will be dealt with in the final chapter.

The woollen trade, centred on Kendal, was well established, with weavers both in the town and throughout the Lakes; as we have already seen it was well served by packhorse routes in every direction, and the first record of a stage coach to London was in 1658, though this did not become a regular service until the following century.

In medieval times, the roads seem to have maintained themselves, helped, no doubt, by occasional assistance from the Church and the monasteries. After the dissolution, and with the growth of trade in Tudor England, Parliament passed an Act in 1555 by which road maintenance was ordered to be undertaken by each parish. Every year each parish had to elect someone to survey the roads, and he had then to report on their condition and to see that necessary repairs were done by the parishoners themselves under his supervision. In 1691 Parliament further enacted that roads should be of a minimum standard; those leading to market towns should be even, level and at least eight feet wide, whereas 'horse causeys' (ie packhorse tracks) should be not less than three feet wide.[1] Needless to say, this system did not work well, and by the eighteenth century the county authorities were gradually assuming the maintenance of many of the bridges, and some of the roads, along the main routes.

Around Kendal the local authorities paid some attention to their roads; in 1669 it was ordered that owners of land on either side of the North Road should 'cut and flash their hedges hanging into the way under pain of 10/- each', while in 1703 the surveyors were required to 'sufficiently repair the highways and enlarge the same where necessary . . . as so to make them good and sufficient for the passage of coaches, carts and carriages'.[2] In 1712 there was a local order to erect signposts at crossroads to guide travellers from one market to the next.

Benjamin Browne, High Constable of Kendal, carried out two surveys of the bridges and roads in his Ward; the first was done in 1712, and is mainly concerned with the bridges — several of which needed repairs. His survey of the highways, done in 1730-1, is often quoted; he evidently surveyed fifteen roads in Kendal Ward, from Beetham through to Grasmere, but he has nothing good to say about any of them; for example: 'Preston Patricke from Crooklands Bridge to Farleton Bridge severall places of it is very Narrow and very much covered with Hassell [Hazel] and Thorn etc'. The narrowness of the roads is his chief complaint, though most are also described as 'bad' or 'covered with ye hedges'.[3] This narrowness reinforces Celia Fiennes's view of the Kendal to Bowness road in 1697 (chapter 5), but at least the fact that surveys were being carried out suggests that there was some concern about the roads, though it could simply be the case that only the statutory obligations were being carried out, and little improvement was being made. We only know of the surveys anyway because of the chance survival of the Browne manuscripts. One final point also needs making; the surveyor was interested in noting the bad roads, not the good ones, and thus we should not be surprised to see that only the former are recorded. After all, anyone reading today's Law Reports might get a picture of unrelieved crime, whereas most people are clearly not criminals. The Browne road survey cannot thus be relied on to give the whole picture about the state of the roads.

Despite this, it is evident that many roads were inadequate for the rapid growth of traffic during the eighteenth century and it became clear to those with an economic interest in the area, principally the major landowners and traders, that something had to be done.

6.2 Early Turnpikes

The first turnpike act in England was passed in 1663 for a section of the Great North Road in the counties of Hertford and Huntingdon; this established for the first time the principle that travellers should contribute towards the repair of roads. The next act was not passed until 1695, but the idea evidently then caught on so that by 1730 there were already ninety turnpike trusts with over 2,000 miles of roads. However, the real boom was to come in the turnpike 'mania' between 1751 and 1772 when over 400 trusts were established, bringing the total mileage to over 15,000.[4] This expansion clearly formed part of the beginning of the Industrial Revolution. The establishment of what has been referred to as the turnpike *system* was essentially a local affair; it was not planned by central government in any way, but by local landowners, merchants, manufacturers, town councils and indeed anyone else who was interested in improving the roads and thus facilitating travel and trade. Occasionally there was local opposition from farmers, drovers, carriers (especially in the packhorse trade) or local traders who thought that the new roads would harm their interests, either by altering the established pattern of markets, or by raising costs because of the tolls to be imposed.

Turnpike trusts were intended to be temporary bodies which would be

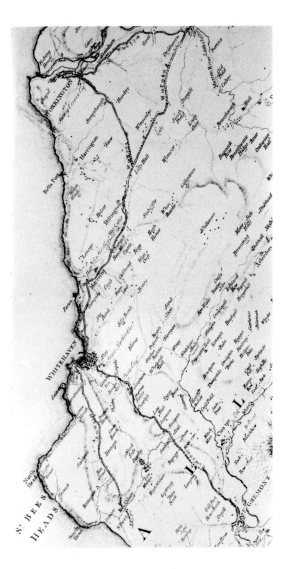

Fig 6.1   Whitehaven turnpikes – Donald, 1774

dissolved when the roads had been improved and when the creditors had been paid. Turnpike acts lasted for only twenty-one years — thus emphasising their temporary nature, and they then had to be renewed. Very few trusts ever dissolved themselves voluntarily, and renewal became virtually automatic, for if a trust kept its roads well and also had no debts, that was a clear sign of good management and was thus to be encouraged.

Turnpikes generally took over existing roads and simply improved the worst parts, though in hilly areas entirely new stretches of road occasionally had to be built, as the earlier tracks had steep gradients suitable only for foot-passengers or packhorses. In the eighteenth century there were no great advances in the techniques of road building, and so improvements were limited to little more than filling potholes and ruts, or digging drainage ditches. There was however, one important change, namely that the multiplicity of older routes, especially over open land or hills, was reduced to a single line of travel.

Whitehaven   The first turnpikes in Cumbria were created quite late on in the process — over a hundred already existed elsewhere in the country before the

Whitehaven turnpikes were established in 1739. These roads are a special case, for they were not designed to link in with other roads, but simply to serve the hinterland of the growing port and town of Whitehaven. In fact, their creation has been overlooked by several writers because they were created in an act to improve the harbour, which was itself intended to update earlier acts of 1709 and 1712. The *Commons Journal* records some of the difficulties of travel reported to the House: 'And the said Witnesses, being further examined, said, that the several Roads leading to Whitehaven . . . are very narrow and deep . . . and that a single Horseman, in many Parts thereof, cannot pass by a Cart or laden Horse'. The earlier improvements in the harbour had evidently increased local trade so much as to put far too great a strain on the existing roads bringing coal and other goods into the town. The act's preamble states its aims: 'For preserving and inlarging the Harbour of Whitehaven in the County of Cumberland; and for repairing and amending the High Roads leading to the said Harbour and Town of Whitehaven'.

The roads are described as follows:

> from Egremond, over Bigrig Moor, to Scalegil, and so to Whitehaven, and from the Town of St. Bees to Whitehaven, and from a place called Bridgefoot, over Clifton and Winscales Moors, to Dissington, and so to Whitehaven, and from the Whin-house at the East End of Harrington, over Workington Moor, to Dissington aforesaid. . . .[6]

The roads can be seen on Donald's map of 1774 though the last branch is shown going through to Workington itself (Fig 6.1). The fifty-seven Trustee Commissioners (beginning with Sir James Lowther) were empowered to erect turnpikes (strictly speaking the word refers to the actual *gate* at the toll house), to collect tolls, to widen and repair the roads and so on — indeed the details of how the trust was to be operated cover almost twenty pages, compared to only four pages devoted to the harbour.

In 1748 the *Gentleman's Magazine* was able to assert that these roads were 'every day improving' and were 'equal to the best Turnpikes around London'. The success of the venture may well have encouraged others in the area to create more new roads, though turnpikes were also reaching towards Cumbria from Newcastle, York and Lancaster. Six separate turnpike Acts were passed in 1753 alone, and a further six had been set up by 1767. This remarkably short period of time constitutes the 'turnpike mania' in and around the Lake District; no more were created until 1794.

It might be thought that compiling a list of the turnpike Acts and their routes would be simple and routine — but the most obvious source for Cumbria (Williams) has a woefully inadequate list and map, while the national lists given in Albert and Pawson often give little idea of the detailed routes — for example what these two authors list as 'Kendal to Sedbergh, etc' and 'Sedbergh roads ' respectively in fact include three separate routes. The next problem is that most Acts were only made for a limited number of years, and had to be renewed — but these later Acts, which often included powers for new lengths of road, are not given in any of the published lists. Finally, it is evident that some turnpike Acts were never implemented and thus the following list cannot simply be taken at face value.

Cumbrian Turnpike Trusts 1739-67 (The stages in brackets were not implemented)

Whitehaven	1739
Bowes-Brough	1743
(Egremont Salthouse, Duddon Bridge, Santon bridge)	1750

Richmond-Lancaster	1751
Preston-Lancaster-Heron Syke	1751
Newcastle-Carlisle	1751
Brough-Eamont Bridge	1753
(Carlisle)-Cockermouth-Workington	1753
Keighley-Kirkby Lonsdale-Kendal	1753
Carlisle-Eamont Bridge	1753
Heron Syke-Eamont Bridge	1753
Penrith-Chalk Beck	1753
Kendal-Milnthorpe, Dixies-Clawthorpe	1759
Appleby-Kendal, Orton-Shap, Tebay-Brough	1761
Hesket-Cockermouth-Keswick-Kendal-Windermere, Keswick-Penrith	1762
Kirkby Stephen-Sedbergh-Greta Bridge, Sedbergh-Kendal, Sedbergh-Grayrigg	1762
Kendal-Kirkby Ireleth	1763
Carlisle-Skillbeck	1767

All this is more clearly seen in map form (Fig 6.2) where the progress of turnpiking and the *ad hoc* growth of a useful network are evident. Soon after the creation of the Whitehaven roads another act was passed for the road across Stainmore to Brough in 1743, and in 1751 a turnpike reached Lancaster from the south, and was carried on to the old county boundary at Heron Syke, as well as to Richmond in Yorkshire. The Military Road from Newcastle to Carlisle, already described in chapter 4, was begun in 1751. Of course it took many years to implement the provisions of a turnpike Act, we have already seen references to turnpikes still under construction or in poor condition in the writings of Arthur Young and Thomas Gray. For example, both of them travelling in about 1770 recorded unfinished sections of turnpike between Ambleside, Windermere and Kendal — the Act for which had been passed in 1762. Some turnpikes, however, never seem to have been constructed at all — an early example is a whole string of roads south of Egremont, the Act for which was passed in 1750 and again in 1762. It specifies a road to Gosforth (with a branch to Santon Bridge), Ravenglass, two ways to Bootle, and then on to Whicham where the route divides — one going to Salthouse (now Millom) to cross the estuary, the other going around, and ending at Duddon Bridge.[7] The preamble says that these roads needed to be improved because of the increased number of wagons and carts travelling to and from Whitehaven. It even describes the route via Salthouse as part of the 'Kings High Road' from Lancaster and Kendal, and Sir James Lowther appears again as the first of the trustees. Perhaps this is an example of over enthusiasm; the trustees grossly over-estimated the revenues that would be obtained from such a remote and relatively little used route. The existing turnpike was eventually extended the four miles to Calder Bridge but nothing more had been done by 1806, when a petition was made to Parliament for a Bill to improve the same roads. It was unsuccessful, and in 1824 the *Whitehaven Gazette* printed a letter asking for the turnpike to be extended: 'It would be a great relief to the inhabitants of this district if the turnpike road could be extended from Calder Bridge to Ravenglass.'[8] It never was.

The remoteness of this whole area probably meant that anyone wanting to travel from any of the West Cumberland ports to distant places such as Glasgow, Dumfries, Liverpool or even Carlisle would have considered going by sea — it was both faster and cheaper, though a little less pleasant and certainly less safe, especially in winter. This possibility also partly explains the late and limited development of turnpikes from the coastal area through to the main towns inland.

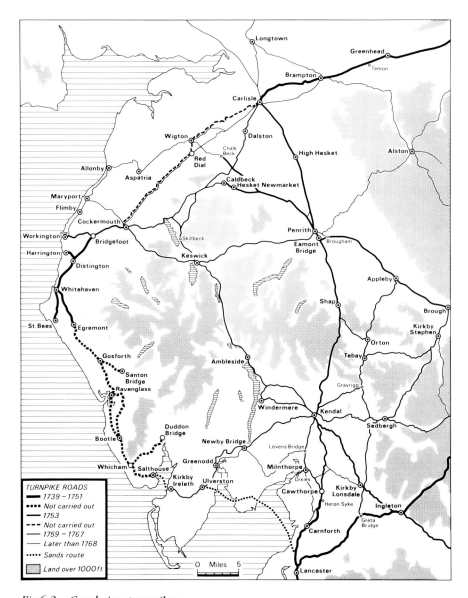

Fig 6.2   Cumbrian turnpikes

6.3   Shap and the Other 1753 Turnpikes

1753 saw the passage of no less than six turnpike Acts for what is now Cumbria, totalling about 140 miles. Briefly summarised, they included roads from Heron Syke and Keighley to Kendal, and on over Shap to Eamont Bridge; from Brough to Eamont Bridge and Carlisle; from Penrith to Chalk Beck; and lastly from Carlisle to Workington (Fig 6.2). They will be described in that order.

The Act for the road north from Lancaster as far as the old county boundary at Heron Syke had been passed in 1751; from here the new road continued to Kendal, meeting the other new turnpike from Keighley and Kirkby Lonsdale (B6254) via Old Hutton, barely a mile before the centre of Kendal. The crossing of the Shap Fells was the major obstacle facing this road; and the need for its improvement had been highlighted by the difficulties encountered by both armies

142

Heron Syke on the A6070 – the old county boundary

in the 1745 rebellion. Things had been little different a hundred years earlier when three Norwich soldiers journeyed from Penrith to Kendal 'through such wayes, as we hope we neuer shall againe, being no other than climing and stony and nothing but bogs and myres and the tops of those high hills, so as wee were enforc'd to keepe these narrow, loose, stony, base wayes though neuer soe troublesome and dangerous. . . . On wee went for . . . the space of 8 miles travelling a slow marching pace. . . .'[9]

The first turnpike route simply followed the old medieval track, though traces of other old routes have been identified by W. Withers who suggests a Bronze Age date for them.[10] They are, however, more likely to be remnants of the multiple lines of travel which developed in hilly areas during medieval times.

It is now a fascinating trip to follow the original Shap turnpike route which had to be largely re-aligned in the 1820s, in order to ease the gradients for heavy or fast traffic; the old and new lines are shown in Fig 6.4. A copy of Jefferys's map of 1770 (Fig 6.3) and a 1:25,000 OS map are useful for following this route. The A6 is certainly a pleasurable road now that virtually all the through traffic goes via the M6. Two sections of the old route — namely Otter Bank to Watchgate and Hollowgate to Hause Foot — can still be driven, but the rest has reverted to the province of the foot traveller. The old and new roads coincide as far as Otter Bank (532972), but from there the old road went directly over the hill to Watchgate. The present line of the A6 was built in 1822 and was described in the *Westmorland Advertiser* thus: 'The first alteration of the road takes place about 4 miles north of Kendal, avoids the narrow lane through the village of Gateside, passes the ravine of Bannisdale Beck by an embankment and an immensely high bridge, of a single arch, and joins the old road again near Forest Hall.' A mile further on 'a second deviation has amazingly improved the ascent from Hollowgate and the descent to High Burrow-bridge'.[11] In 1826 the trustees requested Mr McAdam to make a plan and estimate of an entirely new road between Hollowgate and the summit, including a new bridge, now known as Huck's Bridge; one of the adjacent houses was formerly the Bay Horse Inn.

▲ The old Shap turnpike behind the Plough Inn

▲ Huck's Bridge. High Borrow Bridge can be seen beyond

◄ Fig 6.3   Shap – Jefferys, 1770

The old road here can be followed from just beyond the old Jungle Cafe (548027); it climbs steadily, gaining 300ft in height before dropping down to the now little-used High Borrow Bridge (550040). The road continues up Crookdale for another mile to the equally deserted farm of Hause Foot. From here the road (now only a footpath but still 20ft wide and well engineered) climbs in a single large zig-zag to its summit at about 1,465ft, some 80ft higher than the later road, built across the moss which the earlier road had sought to avoid. Both these roads climb considerably higher than the M6 in crossing these fells — the motorway summit is at only 1,036ft. The correspondent to the paper continued his description: 'Soon after passing the summit a third alteration, deviating to the right[?] and crossing Wasdale beck by a new bridge misses the Dennings and

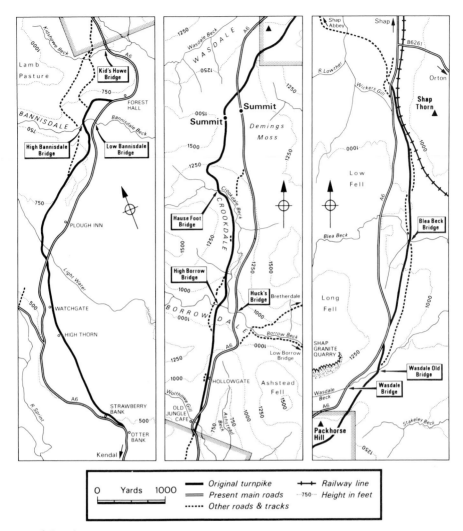

Fig 6.4   Shap routes

Legend:
- Original turnpike
- Present main roads
- Other roads & tracks
- Railway line
- 750 Height in feet
- 0   Yards   1000

Wasdale-bridge Mills, and it is hoped that this deviation will be continued so as to avoid the Blea beck bridge and Wickerslack hills, and afterwards rejoin the old road near the new toll-bar'.

All this was duly done, and the road which had caused so much trouble in the past and had been the greatest challenge taken on by any of the turnpike engineers, was at last capable of taking heavy and fast traffic over this difficult route. Unfortunately, the opening of the railway over Shap in 1846 took away much of this road's valuable traffic so that the annual tolls collected at Bannisdale and Shap fell from around £240 in 1841 to £93 in 1852 and to only £48 in 1875. This was to prove the basic reason for the demise of the trusts — but that is another story, and in any case they had improved the main roads of England out of all recognition. Anyone wishing to read about the history of the trusts in the nineteenth century is referred to L.A. Williams's book.[12]

The main road from Yorkshire over Stainmore, for the most part still following the old Roman route, had received its turnpike Act as far as Brough in 1743, and it too was continued to Eamont Bridge in 1753. The original line of the Roman road

Crookdale. The original turnpike follows the valley bottom while the 1826 route slants up the side of the valley

for two miles either side of Brough is not known, but it is likely to have gone directly into and out of the Roman fort half a mile south of the medieval market town. The turnpike evidently rejoins the Roman line near Brough Hill — the cattle fair ground — and continues along it until Coupland, two miles before Appleby where the old main road (now the B6542) turns off the new by-pass (along the Roman line!) to reach the county town, situated just across the River Eden.

Hause Foot. The original surface of the turnpike is still intact here, just before the road makes its final climb to the summit

Wasdale Old Bridge

In 1824 plans were drawn up to re-align the turnpike into and out of Appleby, to shorten the route and also to reduce the ups and downs. For example, the proposed new line between Brough and Appleby, though only 130yd shorter than the old, would have reduced the total of rises and falls from 1,343ft to only 543 ft. Part of the proposal can be seen in Fig 6.5; the new road from Brough was to take a totally new course — shown by the plot numbers 50-67 which indicate the ownership of different fields along the new route. An existing lane — Draw Bridge Lane — was to be used for the final approach to Appleby. Beyond the town the new route was to rejoin the Roman road earlier than before, missing Crackenthorpe entirely. Indeed it is clear that the whole length of the Roman road past Appleby was still in use at this date. None of these deviations was ever built, and the main road still went much the same way until the new by-pass was constructed.

The turnpike and the modern road then rejoin the Roman line as far as Brougham, but here the three diverge. The Roman and modern roads cross the River Eamont here, but the original turnpike went on to cross the rivers at Lowther Bridge and Eamont Bridge, a mile upstream, where it met the road coming north from Shap. The later trunk road and bridge between Brougham and Penrith were

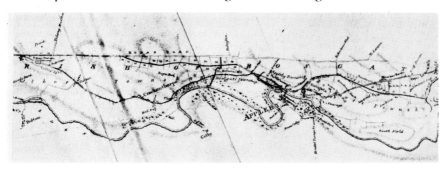

Fig 6.5   Appleby: 1824 turnpike proposals

Roads at Brougham. The medieval castle (right) and the Roman fort (behind it) can be seen. The original turnpike ran across the back; the bridge on the right was part of the 1812 turnpike, and has been superceded in turn by a newer bridge.

only created by an Act of 1812 and this turnpike, only 1½ miles long, was one of the shortest ever built.

From Eamont Bridge the continuation of the Shap turnpike led directly on through Penrith to Carlisle, following the Roman line virtually all the way. The original turnpike led straight out of Penrith, and up the hill to join the Roman line at about 508325, and then down to what is now a large roundabout. In 1825 this first section was by-passed by using the existing road to Hutton as far as Milestone House, and then building a new section of road as shown in Fig 6.6 and thus cutting out the hill, even though it had involved a climb of less than 200ft. There is a minor diversion from the Roman line at Plumpton, and a by-pass has now been built around High Hesket. After crossing Wragmire Moss the Roman line is left again, this time for two miles, as far as Carleton, but various alterations proposed for this section in 1825 were never carried out (Fig 6.7).

Back at Penrith, another turnpike was authorised to Chalk Beck — hardly an obvious or well-known spot. In fact Chalk Beck is a small stream which flows eventually into the Wampool, and the road crosses it very close to the cattle fair ground at Rosley (326450). It may have been intended to end the road there, but it was more likely that the route was intended to continue to Wigton, and that the last five miles did not need improving. Most of this turnpike is now the B5305. In addition there was to be a branch leading to Caldbeck.

The final Act passed in 1753 was for a turnpike from Carlisle to Workington, which would link up with the Whitehaven roads. The route proposed was a curious one, at least as far as Wigton, for instead of following the Roman line, it was to pass through 'Raffles, Kell Houses, Wood House and Micklethwaite'. This route is clearly shown on Donald's map of 1774. It was then to join the Roman road at Red Dial and follow it to Bothel and Papcastle, then across the river to

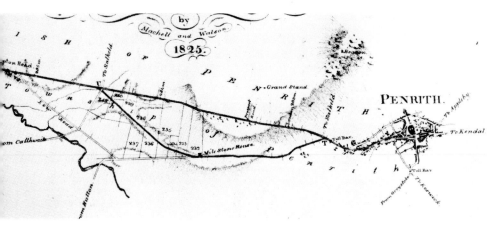

Fig 6.6   Penrith: 1825 turnpike proposals

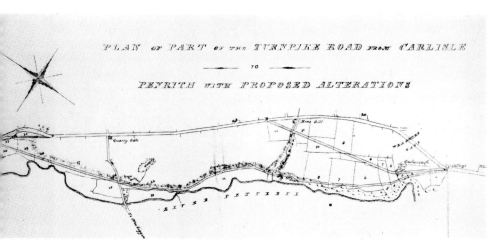

Fig 6.7   Wragmire: 1825 turnpike proposals

Fig 6.8   Cockermouth to Bothel: 1808 proposals

Cockermouth, and on to Bridgefoot and Workington. When the Act came up for renewal in 1779 it was evident that only the Cockermouth to Workington section had been turnpiked, and the link to Carlisle had been made via the Carlisle to Skillbeck turnpike in 1767 (see below). In the early 1770s there was a scheme for a road through Wigton and Maryport to Workington which came to nothing and in fact the Roman road was not turnpiked until 1824. Even the section from Red Dial to Thursby (avoiding Wigton) was included as a branch route, and there was a proposal which would have created a new route between Cockermouth and Bothel. This is shown on a sketch plan of 1808 (Fig 6.8) with the 'Intended line of Road to Carlisle' going via Isel Hall and Sunderland. It is thus largely a matter of chance that the Roman line is the one which is now the main road.

6.4 Turnpikes Through the Lake District 1759-67
The third stage in turnpiking the roads of the Lake District occupied only nine years, during which over 230 miles of roads were to be improved. These roads fall into three groups: the first being those through the Lakes (with a link to Carlisle), the second being a whole network of roads east of Kendal, and the third being routes south and west of Kendal around Morecambe Bay which will be dealt with separately in the next section.

One of the 1762 Turnpike Acts included four separate roads: Hesket Newmarket to Cockermouth, Cockermouth to Kendal, Kendal to Windermere, and Keswick to Penrith, two of which traversed the centre of the Lake District.

The section from Hesket to Cockermouth may never have been completely turnpiked, it was certainly built from Cockermouth to Ouse Bridge (spelt *Yewes* in the act), ignoring the older road over Setmurthy Common, but whether it was ever fully improved to Uldale and Hesket is uncertain. By the end of the century, the route from Ouse Bridge down the east bank of Bassenthwaite to Keswick had certainly been turnpiked; and provided an easier if longer route than Whinlatter. As we have already seen, Gray reported the section west of Ouse Bridge already completed in 1769, and he said that it was to be contined back to Penrith — though whether he meant by way of Keswick or Hesket is not clear.

The road to Carlisle, as we saw in the last section, linked in with the Cockermouth to Hesket road. From Carlisle it kept to the west of the River Caldew; it is still a straight and wide road for it was laid out across this area when it was still unenclosed common land. It is now the B5299 and it passes through Dalston and

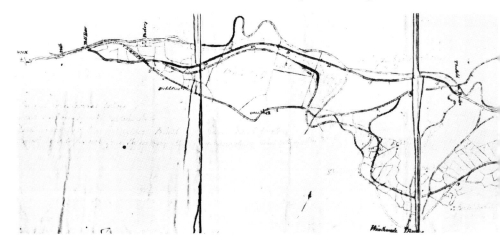

Fig 6.9   Keswick to Threlkeld: 1760 proposals

Keswick Tollhouse

Welton, before crossing the Chalk Beck turnpike at the String of Horses Inn and climbing Warnell Fell (335413). Its route here may at first seem odd, for it has two sharp changes of direction, and climbs 150ft higher than is necessary. The reason for going almost to the top of the Fell was to serve the numerous quarries in the area. Indeed it is likely that the rest of the route was never improved to the same standard. It continues by way of Paddigill (302402) to join the Hesket turnpike at Mulaside (286386). The Act describes the final section of this turnpike as leaving the Hesket turnpike 'between *Binsey Mires* and the *North Raw Gate*' (268377) and proceeding via Bassenthwaite Chapel to its terminus at 'Skillbeck' where another turnpike continued to Keswick. The route is now the minor road through Orthwaite, and Donald's map clearly shows it as such — it did not in fact pass the chapel. The terminus is rather curious — for the most knowledgeable visitor to the Lakes is unlikely to have heard of Skillbeck. It is in fact a small stream crossed by the road near Mire House (235282), and its importance may be due to nothing more than the fact that the parish boundary between Bassenthwaite and Crosthwaite also crosses the road here, the inference being that the road beyond, leading into Keswick, did not need improving.

The original turnpike route between Cockermouth and Keswick was via Lorton and the Whinlatter Pass, rather vividly described by Hutchinson in 1794:

The steeps and alpine passes of Whinlater form an ascent of five miles, up stupendous heights, by a winding path, contrived in an excellent manner, passing round the foot of the mountains . . . to render the advance more gradual. . . . The lake of Bassenthwaite looks from thence like a gloomy abyss, and the vale of Keswick . . . appeared to us an enchanted ground. . . . Skiddaw, shrouded with vapours, appeared to nod his drowsy head.[13]

From Keswick one road was built to Penrith, and we are fortunate that a rough sketch map has survived showing how the engineers hoped to tackle the climb from Keswick to Threlkeld (Fig 6.9). It appears that one road was already in existence, running past Fieldside, Castlerigg Stone Circle, and Goose Well (295238) and then almost direct to Threlkeld Bridge. The surveyors clearly intended to avoid the worst of the climb by keeping close to the top of the gorge of the river Greta, and beyond there were numerous options for crossing the end of St John's in the Vale including going as far south as Wanthwaite Bridge (314231). Two routes were proposed beyond Threlkeld, both on the south side of the River Glendermackin. As was so often the case, when it actually came to building the road, the existing track past the stone circle and on through Threlkeld, Doddick and Scales was the route used. Ten miles were rebuilt by McAdam in 1824, and it remained in use until the major reconstruction of the A66 in the 1970s. Another surviving feature is the former toll house near the railway bridge in Keswick (274238).

East of Scales the route continued through Penruddock and Stainton, but a very complex dispute arose concerning toll gates at the entrance to Penrith. The trust was obliged, under its act, to maintain several minor roads from Greystoke, Newbiggin and Newton, but although they collected tolls from the users of these roads (who were, after all, local people) they neglected to repair the roads. The complexities arose from the building of a second toll gate in 1843 and the re-siting of the original one three years later.[14]

Back at Keswick the turnpike to Ambleside left directly from the centre of the town along what is now a minor road as far as 278232 where it is joined by the present main road (Fig 4.18). The route from here is little changed in essence, although much widened throughout; the climb out of Keswick, described by West as 'somewhat quick' is still steep. Along the shore of Thirlmere, the new road built by Manchester Corporation when they raised the level of the lake by 50ft in the 1880s, is very close to the old one, now beneath the waters. The road then crosses Dunmail Raise, probably the lowest and most frequented of the Lakeland passes. Curiously, the north side of the pass has barely been improved at all, while the long

Dunmail Raise, 1810

Beyond Grasmere the old turnpike ran left, past Dove Cottage, the present main road being built in 1823.

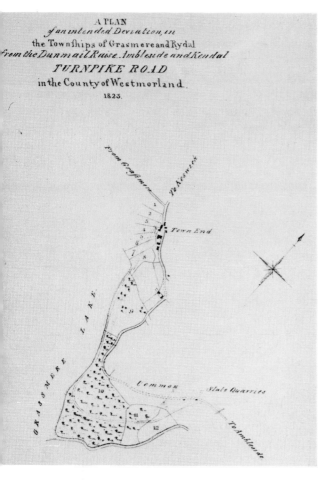

Fig 6.10   Grasmere to Rydal diversion, 1823

153

descent to Grasmere now has a vast width of tarmac. An early nineteenth century print makes the road appear in excellent condition, but it is difficult to relate this rather idealised view to any particular spot in the pass.

The only part of this whole route ever to be significantly altered was between Grasmere and Rydal; the original turnpike went up the narrow lane past Dove Cottage and over the top of the spur called White Moss separating the two lakes. A beautifully drawn little plan illustrates the later diversion which goes along the shore of Grasmere and then through a cutting before rejoining the old route at the car parks overlooking Rydal Water (Fig 6.10). This diversion ought to have upset Wordsworth, for both he and Dorothy used to walk along the shore of Grasmere, and there is still a spot known as Wordsworth's Seat, but by then he no longer lived at Dove Cottage, having moved to Rydal Mount in 1813.

The turnpike was divided into the Ambleside and the Cockermouth-Penrith Trusts in the renewal act of 1824, and the former began to improve its road which had evidently become less than adequate. The White Moss deviation was carried out in 1825-6, in 1828 the section between Ambleside and Bowness was repaired, and the hill at Troutbeck Bridge was eased in 1848.[15]

Beyond Troutbeck Bridge, instead of climbing steeply up the hill to go north of Orrest Head, the turnpike took the present easier route past the top of Windermere town which, needless to say, did not exist in 1762. The remainder of the route to Kendal is generally followed by the present busy A591. At Plumgarths, now obscured beneath the roundabout at the northern end of the Kendal by-pass, the final stretch of turnpike in this Act led westwards through Crook to Windermere, no doubt to link up with the horse-ferry across the lake to Sawrey and Hawkshead.

During the century, Kendal became just as important a centre for stage coach and carrier services as it had formerly been for packhorse traffic. Already by 1763, no less than nine turnpike roads converged on the town, and by 1790, twenty-eight carriers were operating out of the town with services at least once a week to twenty-two places throughout the north of England as well as to London. East of Kendal a whole host of roads were to be turnpiked in Acts passed in 1761 and 1762. Briefly, they led to Appleby (via Tebay and Orton), and to Kirkby Stephen and Brough (via both Tebay and Sedbergh), with cross-roads running from Shap to Orton, and from Grayrigg to Sedbergh, Kirkby Lonsdale and Greta Bridge (Fig 6.2). These roads have all survived more or less intact, and brief descriptions of them have been given by J.F. Curwen.[16]

The only major changes to any of these roads have been on the A685 near Tebay which has been altered in several places recently, first to accommodate the M6 in the Lune gorge, and second between Tebay and Newbiggin on Lune where a brand new road over five miles long has been built along the old railway line. The old road, probably perfectly adequate for the small amount of traffic along this route, is still in use throughout, and the highway authority now has to maintain twice as much road as before. One might have thought it more important to build by-passes around some of the small towns and villages nearby which have extremely busy roads running straight through them (Staveley and Ambleside spring immediately to mind) rather than building vast new roads where there is little traffic. But we are no longer in the days of the turnpikes when roads were improved only if local people were prepared to pay directly for them. No longer are roads a direct expression of the demand for them.

6.5   Turnpikes Around the Sands

The building of turnpikes around Morecambe Bay is essentially a continuation of the story of the route across the sands, and yet it was not until 1820 that a reasonably short alternative route was open to traffic.

Fig 6.11   Kent Estuary – Jefferys 1770

The first turnpike act connected with the sands was passed in 1759, and is given as two routes: from Nether Bridge to Dixies, and Miltrop to Hangbridge. None of these names appears on the modern one-inch or 1:50,000 maps, but Nether Bridge is in Kendal; Dixies is west of Milnthorpe, at Sandside; Miltrop is Milnthorpe itself, and Hangbridge is on the B6384 a mile and a half to the south-east, heading for the existing Heron Syke turnpike at Clawthorpe. The reason for improving these routes so early may not immediately be obvious but in fact Dixies was a port, one of many around the bay, and was the nearest to Kendal. It is first mentioned as 'Milnthorpe haven' in 1558, and continued to be used until the railway viaduct was built in 1857, effectively obstructing the river channel.

The whole area around the mouth of the River Kent can be seen on Jefferys's map of 1770 (Fig 6.11). There was clearly no good road towards Cartmel at that time, apart from the old road through Witherslack. The main road into Furness in the mid-eighteenth century was further north — namely the old packhorse route from Kendal to Newby Bridge and eventually to Ulverston. This route was impassable for vehicles, and an act to improve it was passed in 1763.[17] The list of trustees begins with Lord Strange and Lord Cavendish, and the almost inevitable Sir James Lowther is fourth in the list. The reason for his interest was that the turnpike

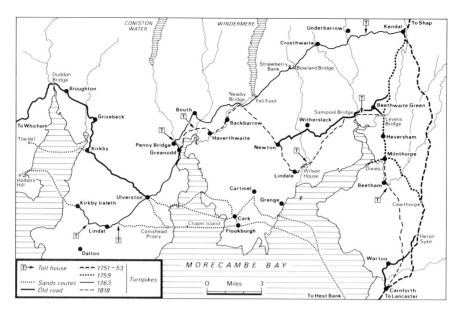

Fig 6.12   Furness Turnpikes

was to end at Kirkby Ireleth, from where the Duddon Sands could be crossed and the coast road (still unimproved) followed to Whitehaven (Fig 6.12). The other advantage of continuing the road beyond Ulverston was to provide a road for the growing iron-mining industry of Low Furness. Both these factors explain why the road did not go to Dalton — once the main market town of the area.

The old packhorse track was evidently widened so that wagons and coaches could use it, but the trust seems to have done little else; the twists and turns of the track were not straightened out, nor were the steep sections eased. Between Kendal and Newby Bridge the current OS map still shows fifteen steep hills; the inn half way up Strawberry Bank has already been noted. West describes this route as 'mountainous and uneven, nevertheless in other respects it affords an agreeable ride'. The road then crossed the river at Newby Bridge and went over what the original act called 'Elingharth Brow' and down into Rusland Valley. Here it crossed the mosses on a causeway, reaching *terra firma* again just before the village of Bouth. It then went on towards Tottlebank, but turned left at 317842 along what is now a very narrow lane to cross the River Crake at Penny Bridge for Greenodd, another of the ports around the bay. The route then continued via Ulverston, Lindal, and Tytup to Kirkby Ireleth, and it is indicative of where the heaviest traffic was expected to be on the turnpike that two of the four toll houses were placed on this final section (ie at Lindal and Tytup).

James Stockdale described a journey over part of this turnpike in 1801; with his parents he had crossed the sands from Cark to Ulverston, but they returned 'by the long and wearisome road round the head of the estuary', because the tide had come in, preventing them returning the same way they had come. It took them an hour to reach Greenodd because the turnpike was so bad, and then they went by Penny Bridge and Bouth to Haverthwaite. Here they had to negotiate the 'rotten wooden bridge over the River Leven before tackling the deeply rutted track up Bigland Brow (the direct route along the mosses to Cark had not then been built). He summed it all up thus: 'A journey of some fifteen miles . . . over narrow and rough roads, wooden bridges, and precipitous hills, occupying about three and a half hours in the performance.'[18]

The Mason's Arms, Strawberry Bank, half-way up the steep zig-zag in the turnpike

Milestone in the Rusland Valley on the 1763 turnpike

Penny Bridge

As we have already seen in the section about the sands route, this first turnpike had little impact on traffic to and from Lancaster, which continued to cross the sands. An intermediate route did exist via Witherslack (Figs 6.11, 6.12) but it was longer and more difficult than crossing the sands.

Thomas West described it in his *Guide*: 'From Millthrop to Levens 2 miles. From thence to the nearer end of the Long causeway, at Beathwaite Green [ie Levens] 1 mile. Thence to the Black Bull in Witherslack 3 miles (which takes you by the foot of Whitbarrow Scar . . .). Thence to Newton (over the hill Tawtup) 4 miles. Thence to Newby-bridge — 3 miles.' The section over Tow Top was described in 1817 as a 'mountainous track which beggars description', and a local farmer kept a team of horses ready to aid travellers, and no doubt his own pocket too. Its 1 in 4 gradient is still formidable today.

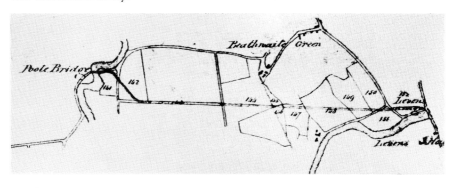

Fig 6.13   Miller's Plan 1817: Levens

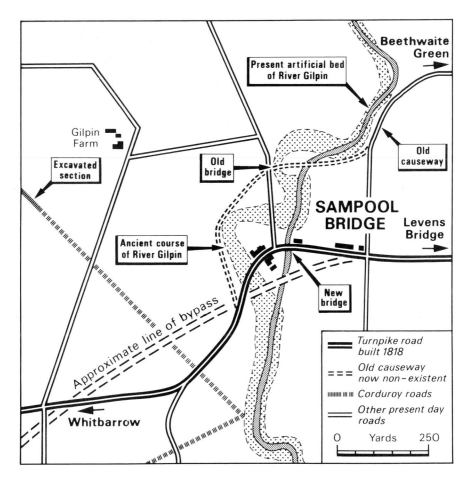

Fig 6.14   Sampool Bridge

Thus it was that another Act was passed in 1818 creating a new route into the Cartmel and Furness peninsulas — it consisted of two detached sections, one from Carnforth to Milnthorpe, and the other from Levens Bridge to Greenodd, the intermediate section having already been turnpiked in 1759.

William Miller was commissioned to produce a map of the whole route showing what existing lanes could be used if widened and straightened, and what new lengths would be needed. This turnpike was unusual in creating long stretches of completely new road; between Levens and Greenodd over half the distance was to be newly laid out. Two sections of his map are shown — the first is the crossing of the mosses between Levens Bridge and Sampool Bridge (Fig 6.13). A new straight line was to be laid out, veering northwards only at the western end to cross the old Lyth Pool Bridge. In fact this bridge was taken down and the present Sampool Bridge built a hundred yards or so farther south. This bridge has been superceded in turn by the new dual carriageway of the A590 (Fig 6.14).

Much of the road over the mosses was in effect 'floated' on bundles of juniper which were cut from the slopes of Whitbarrow Fell. Floating roads across these mosses was not a new technique — bundles of birch or even heather were also used, and part of the area is still known as Stakes Moss no doubt because of this method of road building. Two sections of such 'corduroy roads' were unearthed

The old causeway from
Levens to Pool Bridge

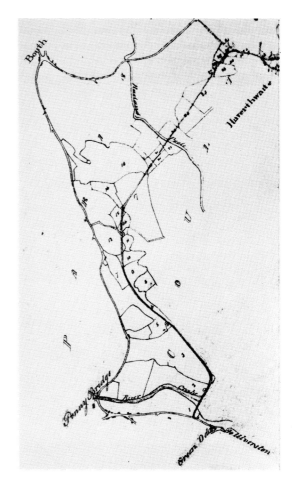

Fig 6.15   Miller's Plan
1817: Bouth to Greenodd

A section of corduroy road excavated about 1900 (CW2, 4 208)

during peat cutting at the turn of the last century.[19] They were made of substantial timbers, and were about 15ft wide. It is quite likely that the old causeway (formerly known as the 'Carsar') running from Levens to Pool Bridge (shown as the existing road in Fig 6.14 was built on similar foundations. J. Briggs, writing in 1825 noted that 'Carriages and the heaviest waggons now pass safely over 4 or 5 miles of morass where, a few years ago, except in very dry weather, the human foot could not tread with security'.[20] For the next three miles most of the old turnpike can still be followed though it no longer carries much traffic. It then ran through Lindale (now by-passed) and up the steep hill towards Newton. At Ayside the turnpike itself by-passed the village, and another new section was created just before Newby Bridge to replace the hilly winding road via Canny Hill.

Fig 6.16   Yates: Carnforth to Beetham, 1786

The turnpike then followed the River Leven to the industrial village of Backbarrow where it crossed the river, and continued to Haverthwaite. The second extract from Miller's map shows the final new section across more mosses and around the tip of Legbarrow Point to Greenodd (Fig 6.15); the 1763 turnpike via Bouth can also be seen.

The section of the road between Carnforth and Milnthorpe also deserves some attention. The Act provided that if the Lancaster to Heron Syke turnpike trust should divert their road so as to go directly from Tewitfield to Carnforth (instead of by Keer Bridge), then the new turnpike could end at Low Hyning, thus saving about two miles; in this event, £1,000 was to be given to the Lancaster to Heron Syke Trust. The roads between Carnforth and Beetham existing before the turnpike can be seen on Yates's map (Fig 6.16). Driving north up the A6 today the alternating old and new sections of the road (as they were in 1820) are clear enough — the longest new section was at Hale Moss, where the road is still straight and wide for well over a mile. The various changes that took place at Beetham can be seen because a detailed map of the area had been drawn in 1733.[21] (Fig 6.17).

The whole turnpike seems to have been built very speedily, and was open throughout by the middle of 1820. The improvements effected in communications, and in particular in postal services, between Furness and the rest of the country in

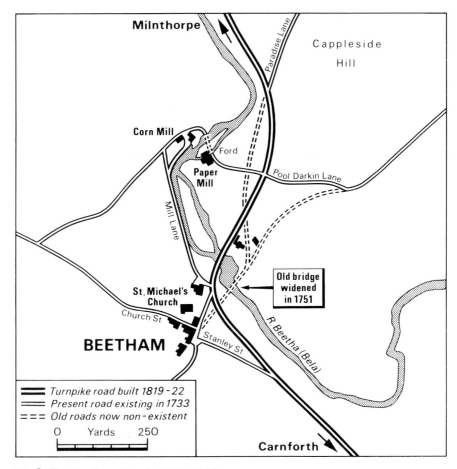

Fig 6.17   Beetham Roads 1733-1820

the eighteenth and nineteenth centuries have been studied in some detail.[22] Perhaps the overall effect can be gauged from the time taken to travel between London and the Lakes:[23]

London to Kendal	1734	9 days	
	1773	3 days	
London to Carlisle	1778	2 days	$3\frac{1}{2}$ hours
	1821	1 day	18 hours
	1825	1 day	10 hours
	1837	1 day	8 hours

In conclusion, it will have become evident that while there was a mania for establishing turnpikes in the 1750s and 1760s, the period between 1815 and 1835 saw not only the establishment of four new turnpikes (Greenodd-Carnforth, Carlisle-Cockermouth, Cockermouth-Maryport, Carlisle-Brampton) but also the expenditure of a vast amount of money on road and bridge repairs. Clearly the toll receipts show a growth in traffic of both merchandise and tourists. However, the turnpike trusts eventually became obsolete (partly due to railway competition), and they were all dissolved between 1870 and 1885, the counties taking over responsibility for the roads as well as for the bridges.

7 Conclusion

7.1 Enclosure Roads

Many hundreds of miles of new roads were created in the early years of the nineteenth century when large areas of Cumbria were enclosed. The enclosing of what had been open land by hedges (or sometimes walls or fences) was part of the move to increase agricultural production, especially during and immediately after the Napoleonic Wars.[1] In much of midland England the medieval open fields around each village had been steadily enclosed since the middle ages, but in Cumbria there were few open fields. It was the commons and waste lands which were enclosed in Cumbria, and brought into cultivation for the first time. Most of this was done by Act of Parliament between 1795 and 1830, with the peak in 1810-15. The net result was the enclosure of 275 thousand acres in Cumberland and Westmorland, representing almost a quarter of the total area of the two counties — an amazingly high figure in view of the fact that much land in the area is too high ever to be farmed.

Professional surveyors were employed to divide up the land among the various landowners, and in the process they often re-drew the whole landscape, including the roads. Major roads usually survived with their routes unchanged, though many of them formerly ran across open ground as can be seen on Ogilby's strip maps (Fig 4.4). The surveyors, wherever possible, drew their field boundaries and roads along new straight alignments. Sometimes old roads were retained, and simply straightened and widened, but many old roads and tracks were destroyed. More land was ploughed up after enclosure, and this has removed most physical traces of earlier tracks.

Considering the fact that so much of England's landscape was re-drawn in this fashion, it is surprising to find how little has been written about enclosure roads; the classic book by W.G. Hoskins *The Making of the English Landscape* devotes only four pages to them, while Christopher Taylor's *Roads and Tracks of Britain* runs to only six.[2] There are dozens of books and many more articles about various aspects of enclosure, but no-one has yet attempted a definitive study of the aspect of enclosure which is most apparent to the modern traveller — namely the roads. Here is another topic crying out for local research; the main requirement is a parish or estate map, dating from before enclosure, and of a sufficiently large scale to show most or all of the roads and trackways across the fields. Sadly, there are very few such maps for our area, but a few can be found in the local Record Offices.

A classic feature is the constant width of enclosure roads — they are often either

164

40 or 50ft wide, much wider than the present day strip of tarmac running down the centre. This is a continuation of a medieval custom that a traveller could diverge from a road if it was impassable, even to the extent of trampling crops; the new enclosed road was still wide enough to allow room for manoeuvre, although the crops were now safe. Enclosed drove roads also tend to be wide, but not as straight, as they cling to the natural contours of the land.

Various improvements to roads have been noted at Crosthwaite, Hutton Roof, and Dalston.[3] Sometimes a road contains elements of both the old and the new — the road north from Cartmel to Fiddler Hall (393850) is a classic example of alternating sections of the old winding road and the four sections straightened out by the enclosure surveyors, who planned a total of twenty-four public carriage roads in their Enclosure Act of 1796. These roads also led to Grange, Newton, Witherslack, Crosthwaite, Bigland and Holker, and in addition there were almost eighty other roads described as private carriageways or driftways; all this was but a part of the complete re-design of an area of about fourteen square miles.

Around Cartmel, rather curiously, the roads were not widened to the usual 40 or 50ft, but to a local 'statute width' of 20ft. Some of them were evidently re-surfaced, including the road over Winder Moor to the Holm (376752) which, it was noted, 'should be covered ten feet wide with broken stones not bigger than a goose's egg,

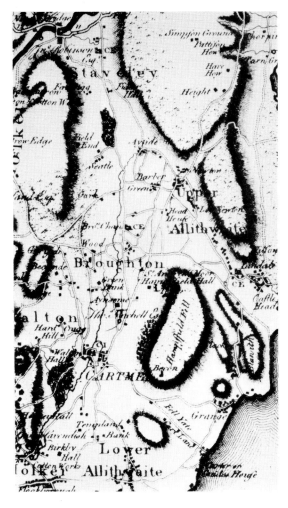

Fig 7.1   Yates: Cartmel, 1786

Milestone near Cartmel

these stones to be nine inches in thickness on the crown of the road'.[4] All this contrasts very sharply with the roads which were little improved, such as the narrow switchback route from Cartmel to High Gate Side (372814), and over Bigland to Low Wood. In effect, the surveyors here kept the old routes, and simply improved them, so that most of the roads shown on Yates's map of 1786 (Fig 7.1) still survive.

There are, however, a few anomalies; writing in 1872 James Stockdale described the road between the Egg-Pudding Stone (394811) and High Newton: 'that part of the road . . . appears exceedingly narrow, as if it had never been made of the same width as the lower part of the road; but on close examination the original walls will still be found standing on each side at the full statute width. Seedling thorns, hazels, and other trees . . . have been fashioned into hedges, a yard wide or more on each side. . . . In fact there is now both a wall fence and a hedge on each side of the road generally!'[5] The road today is even narrower, and the walls have been moved closer together, no doubt to enlarge the fields on either side.

An interesting document survives in the records of the Cavendish family of Holker, dated 1839, which is a 'sketch of roads diverted, stopped up or given up about Holker Hall within the last 60 years'.[5] Part of this area had been affected by the Cartmel Enclosure Act, and a note next to the sketch has some interesting observations on the confused state of responsibility for roads:

> The Commissioners . . . had no power over the Old Roads, or at least they did not interfere with any that were not on the Common; No. 12 was not on the Commons — . . . (it) will therefore be an Ancient Road used by the public but not perhaps repaired by the Public — as is the case with . . . several others. Many of the Commissioners Roads are used by the Public; but are not made or repaired by the Public.

All these roads are shown in Fig 7.2; many of the old tracks can still be followed as footpaths today (for example Nos 1 and 3) though they are often poorly (if at all) signposted or barred by signs saying 'Private Land'. Road 1 had been given up

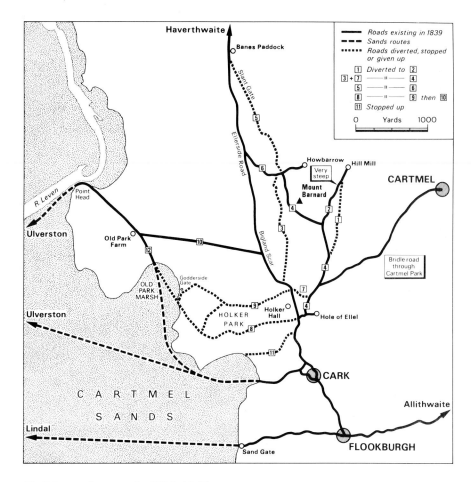

Fig 7.2   Holker Roads, 1780-1840

despite the fact that it had 'very little of a Hill' and replaced by road 2 which had and still has a very steep hill.

The coastline has changed greatly since 1839, largely due to the building of the railway; the document makes this abundantly clear:

> Park Head was a much more frequented Port *once* (nay even within the memory of some men still living) than now. Baltic Vessels used to *winter* there. . . . The only Road then from it to Holker was by no. 12 through Holker Park; the Carke R over the Sands + marshes.

Much more extensive areas of enclosure can be seen by glancing at any of the 1:25,000 maps of the area to the north of Penrith in the area of the great medieval forest of Inglewood. Here the surveyors may have based their main roads on lines originally laid out by the Romans, but most of the roads date from 1819 when 44 square miles were enclosed. Right-angled bends in the roads are particularly common in this area, and these roads also tend to change their alignments at odd places. This is because enclosure of the commons was carried out piecemeal; the first area to be enclosed would have a new straight road direct to a point on the boundary where it would link up with an existing road. When the next area was itself enclosed, the surveyor would plan his road so that it led to the same point on

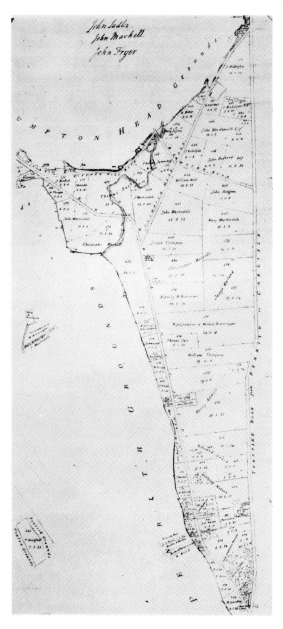

Fig 7.3   Enclosure Map:
          Penrith 1819

the boundary, giving an almost inevitable kink at that spot. Sometimes this coincides with parish boundaries, as at 399379, 419478 or 490475. Fig 7.3 shows the new layout created immediately north of Penrith, before the re-routing of the Carlisle turnpike (see chapter 6), while Fig 7.4 shows a much smaller area around Hutton End (450385). The changes which the surveyors made cannot be fully assessed, for although they must have made maps of the countryside as it was before enclosure, only their plans for the new layout survive. Perhaps a hint of the drastic changes which they wrought can be seen in the area known as Broad Field — the drovers' grazing ground between Carlisle and Penrith. Fig 7.5 shows this whole area as depicted by Donald in 1774 — it was clearly a large open area traversed by unenclosed roads. The area in the centre (marked off by dashed lines)

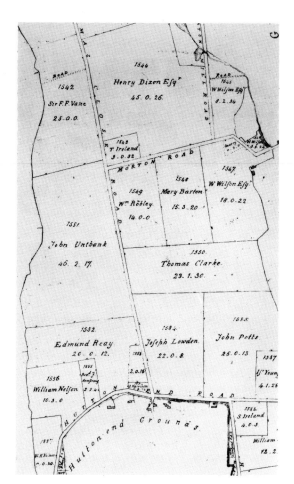

Fig 7.4   Enclosure map:
Hutton End 1819

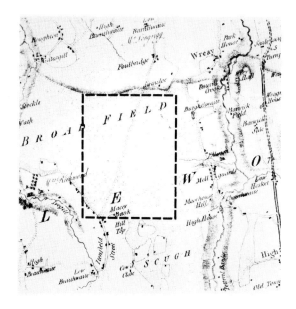

Fig 7.5   Broad Field:
Donald, 1774

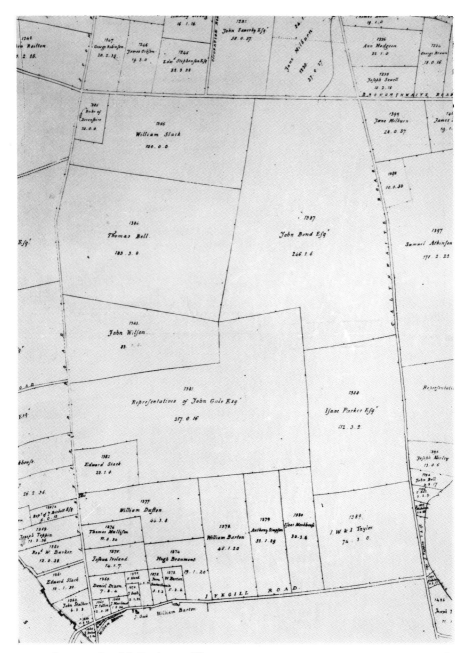

Fig 7.6   Broad Field: Enclosure Plan

is the area covered in the extract from the enclosure plan of 1819 (Fig 7.6); even the single track running across this area before enclosure has not survived.

A little further west similar changes had occurred; 'A line of open commons but a few years since reached from Workington to Carlisle, . . . out of thirty five miles, twenty five at least might have been passed over commons, the whole of which is now enclosed.'[7] The effects were clear enough at the time: 'the first great advantage felt to follow these enclosures was the substitution of stone-made roads

Typical enclosure landscape north of Penrith

Enclosure roads near Reagill (599164)

for the miry and dangerous tracks over the Commons. . . . They . . . afforded freer and easier access to markets, and gradually opened out resources and communications of which the inhabitants had no previous idea, and of which they began to feel the benefits.'[8]

Nevertheless, despite the fact that we are rarely able to see the original road network, the surveyors' handiwork is clear enough, and can be seen in parishes all the way around the Lakeland mountain core, though seldom within it. Enclosure brought about as drastic a change to the local road system as the turnpikes had done to the main roads, and by about 1830 the road network of the Lake District and the surrounding area was much as we know it today.

7.2 Final Thoughts

This last section contains something of a mixture of topics, for as John Norden said in 1607:

> And because that it may be some things be omitted which you now instantly call to mind, blush not to declare it here before you be deprived of that you have written. There may be defects in the forme of your answers yet if you have observed the main purpose which is the seeking out and the delivering the truth, you have discharged [your] honest parts.

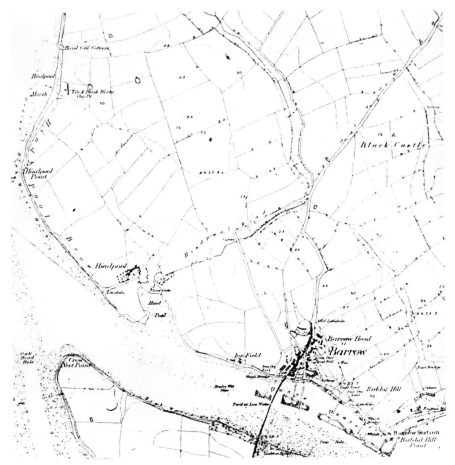

Fig 7.7   Barrow 1851

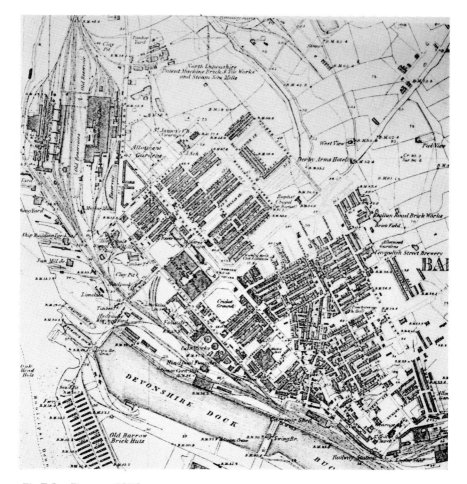

Fig 7.8   Barrow 1873

It will have become clear by now that the story of the growth of the Lakeland road system is virtually complete; only two topics remain — namely the new towns of the nineteenth century and their roads, and the coming of the motor car in the twentieth century.

In the south-west of Cumbria the rapid expansion of the iron industry with the coming of the railways in the middle of the nineteenth century led to the spectacular growth of several towns, principally Millom and Barrow. Just as Whitehaven had been laid out as a planned town with a grid-iron street pattern over a hundred and fifty years earlier, so the roads of these new towns were superimposed on the landscape in the same way. It is interesting to see, however, that some of the old roads have survived. Barrow in 1851 was little more than a tiny fishing village with a lane leading north towards Dalton; the station had only just been built (Fig 7.7). Only twenty-two years later the second edition of the Ordnance Survey map shows a remarkable change, with vast areas given over to industry, housing and railways. But even though the new streets are laid out formally, Dalton Road still survived, and remains as the town's main street to this day (Fig 7.8). The lane which formerly led towards Dalton had by then been widened, and renamed Abbey Road (for it passes close to Furness Abbey), and still provides the town with a wide and impressive approach.

173

Langdale, about 1885, showing the road surface (M. Lefebure)

Road up Borrowdale (M. Lefebure)

The Twentieth Century As late as 1902, Baddeley's guide to *The English Lake District* made no mention of motor vehicles, and it is interesting to see what it says about the roads, and to compare it with later guide-books.[10] Baddeley gives some detail about the roads, with particular reference to both carriage and cycle traffic: 'The carriage road from Boot over the Hard Knott and Wrynose Passes is just traversable by vehicles, but a snare to cyclists.' Not all the roads were passable however: 'Honister Pass is so rough and steep on the Buttermere side as to be practically insurmountable . . . the attempt [to ascend it], we believe is not often made.' Honister did though form the highlight of a round trip from Keswick, ascending from the Borrowdale side.

Referring to the road from Ambleside to Kirkstone the guide makes a general point: 'Like most Lake District roads which follow the course of the old packhorse roads, [it] is so badly engineered as to be rather a succession of jerks than a steep hill in the ordinary sense of the word.' There were some short lengths of new road, however, such as the one from Skelwith Bridge to Elterwater (1½ miles) replacing the steeper route via Loughrigg Tarn. But beyond Chapel Stile and into Langdale itself the guide notes that 'the road falls off in quality'.

Of the main roads, the Windermere to Keswick route had an excellent surface throughout, and had regular coach and waggonette services. The map accompanying the guide is of great interest; it shows most of the mountain passes as pony tracks, and the guide describes Rossett Gill as the roughest. The map shows that virtually all present-day roads were then already in existence. One of the few exceptions is the new road along the eastern shore of Haweswater which replaced the older road on the opposite shore which was flooded when the level of the lake was raised to become a reservoir in the 1930s. The same process had already happened when Thirlmere was enlarged in the 1880s, but in this case new roads were built on both sides of the lake.

The Ward Lock Guide of 1918 clearly shows the impact of the motor car on the area, and gives an outline of the main motor routes: 'Through the energetic action of the County Councils nearly all the main highways are now in good order'. But life was still not without its hazards: 'Motorists are warned that should the car run away with them, as it may, not everyone can have the luck to charge a stone wall, knock it down, have the car turn over on him, and then be well enough to crawl out, photograph the car, and walk healthily on to the hotel. This has actually occurred on this route [Kirkstone] but it is unwise to expect a recurrence of miracles'. It is a pity that we do not have the photograph! Honister too was difficult, and the guide is quite blunt: 'This route is not for motorists'. However, both Honister and the Wrynose-Hard Knott routes were regarded as suitable for hardier cyclists: the improving and surfacing of these roads had not then been started.

The story of the roads over the last sixty years is one of continuing improvement; few new roads have been built, but existing ones have been surfaced with tarmac, widened, straightened, made into dual carriageways, had their gradients eased, and so on. In the south the A590, which survived virtually unaltered along its turnpike route until the 1970s, is at last being upgraded; in the north a new major route has been driven through the National Park, despite much opposition, to link Penrith, Keswick, Cockermouth and the coast (largely along the line of the old A66), and restrictions have been placed on heavy lorries using Dunmail Raise. Last, but not least, the M6, completed in 1971, now carves its way from Lancaster to Carlisle, passing through the Lune Gorge, very close to the Roman fort, and then crossing Shap by a route previously taken (give or take a mile) by the Roman road, several drove roads and turnpikes, and the railway. It has brought 20 million people within a three-hour drive of the Lake District. All this recent development has scarcely altered the road network depicted on the first Ordnance Survey maps just over a hundred years ago. It simply means that people can now reach the Lake District much more easily than ever before, but thereby bringing with them all the modern problems of congestion, especially at the popular summer weekends. Many visitors to the Lakes dash from place to place to admire this, photograph that, or climb up the other — with little regard to the actual routes they are using and which have been in use for hundreds or thousands of years.

Finally, it has to be re-iterated that the subject of this book rests on a rather limited amount of local research. Much work remains to be done on the history of roads — whether of Roman, medieval, Tudor, Stuart, turnpike or enclosure date. If this book encourages anyone (whether a local or a visitor) to look in detail at roads of a particular date, or better still, at roads in a particular area or parish, then it will have been successful. The range of sources given in the references will give some idea of the types of written evidence available, and it is then up to the individual to follow up clues both in the literature and in the field. If your researches prove successful, then you should ensure at least that a copy of your findings is kept by one of the Record Offices, and at best, aim for publication in the Cumberland and Westmorland Antiquarian and Archaeological Society Transactions. This will enable future writers about the development of Lakeland roads and trackways to be more precise than is possible at the moment, and this may in turn encourage those who write about the Lakes not to ignore the roads entirely. For although Lakeland's roads and trackways have been neglected in the past, this book has tried to show that they are a vital part of the landscape and history of this fascinating corner of England.

Acknowledgements

The staff of the Record Offices at Carlisle, Kendal, Barrow and Preston were most helpful, as were those at the excellent Local History Library in Kendal. The Library of Salford University patiently obtained many obscure references, and the Audio-Visual Department did an excellent job of preparing the photographs and reductions of old maps. All the photographs were taken by the author, although the aerial shots could not have been obtained without the assistance of Steve Figures of Denby Dale and his flying machine.

The maps drawn specially for this book are the work of Gustav Dobrzynski, Cartographer in the Department of Geography, University of Salford, who has once again struggled successfully to convert the author's rough sketches into clear and artistic maps. The author's manuscript was even rougher than his sketches, and the two secretaries in the same department, Marie Partington and Moira Armitt cannot be praised highly enough for translating the original scribbles into typewritten form.

Cumbria County Council has been generous in allowing me to reproduce so many of the maps from its various Record Offices; the maps involved are Figs. 4.16, 4.17, 4.18, 4.19, 4.20, 5.3, 5.10, 6.1, 6.3, 6.5, 6.6, 6.7, 6.8, 6.9, 6.10, 6.11, 6.13, 6.15, 7.3, 7.4, 7.5, 7.6. Molly Lefebure has also given me permission to use two photographs from her collection which first appeared in *Cumbrian Discovery* (1977).

Finally, chapter 2 was read by Richard Bellhouse and Geoff Brunstrom, chapters 4 and 5 by Bill Rollinson, part of chapter 7 by Barrie Gleave, and the remainder by Charles Nocton; they all made detailed, valuable and helpful suggestions. The author's deepest thanks are due to *all* those who have helped him to write this book. Needless to say, any errors of fact, omission or emphasis which have crept in are his responsibility alone.

References

Abbreviations

The numerous articles referred to in the *Transactions of the Cumberland and West-morland Antiquarian and Archaeological Society* are indicated by the abbreviations *CW1* (Old Series, 1866-1900) and *CW2* (New series, 1901 to date). To save further space, the *titles* of articles in these transactions are not given. For the rest, the titles of books and journals are in *italics*, with the titles of articles in journals in 'quotes'.

Useful general texts for background reading include:
J. C. Barringer, *The Geography of Lakeland* (1976)
R. Millward and A. Robinson, *The Lake District* (1970); *Cumbria* (1972)
W. Rollinson, *A History of Man in the Lake District* (1967);
   A History of Cumberland and Westmorland (1978)
L. A. Williams, *Road Transport in Cumbria in the Nineteenth Century* (1975)

Chapter 1

1   For the references given in this book, if the *fourth* number of a six figure reference is 0,1,2,3,4,5, or 6, then the prefix is **NY**. Where the fourth number is 7,8, or 9, the prefix is **SD**. Thus Staveley Church is **SD**469986, while Kentmere Church is NY456041. In order to obtain the correct 2½in (1:25,000) map, simply take the letters and the first and fourth numbers, so that Staveley is on sheet SD49 and Kentmere on NY40. The only exceptions occur in the extreme west, around Whitehaven, where the *first* number is 9; here the prefix is **NX**.

Chapter 2

1   S. Frere, *Britannia; A History of Roman Britain*, (1978), especially 123-93
     T. W. Potter, *CW Research Ser* **1** ((1979) 356-9
2   A.L.F. Rivet & C. Smith, *The Place-Names of Roman Britain*, (1979)
3   W.C. Sellar & R.J. Yeatman, *1066 and All That*, (1930) 12
4   F. Haverfield, *CW2*, **19**, (1919) 28-9
5   O. Cuntz, *Itineraria Romana*, (Leipzig, 1929)
     A.L.F. Rivet and C. Smith, *op cit*, 170-2
6   I.D. Margary, *Roman Roads in Britain*, (1973) especially 17-33, 385-99, 496-519
     See also: O.G.S. Crawford, *Man and His Past* (1921) 163-207
7   Thanks are due to P.A. Wilson for preparing a paper on High Street, summarising much previous research in 1976, and more recently to R.G.W. Brunstrom for re-kindling an interest in this route; many of the ideas about the southern end of High Street are his.
8   F.W. Ragg, *CW2*, **10** (1910) 436-8. The spelling varies: also Brestrett, Brethstrede and Bredestrete. The name could also be derived from the Old Norse *breidr*, meaning 'broad'.
9   A. Wainwright, *The Far Eastern Fells*, (1957)
10   F. Haverfield, *CW1*, **15**, (1899) 361ff
11   T. Hay, *CW2*, **43** (1943) 25-27. See also **38** (1938) 43ff
12   R.G. Collingwood, *CW2*, **37** (1937) 1-9
13   T. Hay, *CW2*, **39**, (1939) 17-18
14   R.G. Collingwood, *CW2*, **30** (1930) 118; *CW2*, **13** (1913) 143-6; *CW2*, **64** (1964) 94ff
15   R.G. Collingwood, *CW2*, **21** (1921) 24-9
16   M.E. Burkett, *CW2*, **66** (1966) 477-8
17   I.A. Richmond, *CW2*, **49** (1949) 15-31

18   T. Clare, *Archaeological Sites of the Lake District,* (1981) 39-45
19   C.R.B. McGilchrist, *CW2,* **19** (1919) 17-28
20   J. Horsley, *Britannia Romana* (1732) 482-3
      T. West, *Guide to the Lakes* (1778) 147-54
      R.L. Bellhouse, *CW2,* **54** (1955) 17-27. See also *CW2,* **56** (1957) 28-36
21   ibid, **54,** 20
22   G.G.S. and A. Richardson, *CW2,* **80** (1980) 160-2. The first map reference on p162
      should presumably read NY 403094, and in the penultimate sentence the direction
      should read *north-east.*
23   T. Hay, *CW2,* **37** (1937) 53-4
24   F.W. Ragg, *CW2,* **18** (1918) 151
25   F. Villey, *CW2,* **37** (1937) 49-51
26   T. Wilson, *CW1,* 7 (1883-4) 90
27   P. Ross, *CW2,* **20** (1920) 1-15
28   Rivet and Smith, *op cit,* 157-64
29   R.G. Collingwood, *CW2,* **37** (1937) 9-12
30   Ordnance Survey, *Hadrian's Wall*
31   R.L. Bellhouse and G.G.S. Richardson, *CW2,* **82** (1982) 47-50
32   R.L. Bellhouse, *CW2,* **52** (1953) 41-5. See also G.G.S. Richardson, *CW2,* **72** (1972)
      330
33   E. Birley, *CW2,* **51** (1951) 30-1
34   R.L. Bellhouse, *CW2,* **56** (1957) 37-51
35   *ibid,* 51-6, But see also *CW2* **60** (1960) 24
36   J.B. Bailey, *CW2,* 4 (1904) 250
37   E. Birley, *CW2,* **51** (1951) 35-7
38   A. Richardson, *CW2,* **82** (1982) 67-71; See also: O.A.W. Dilke, *The Roman Land
      Surveyors* (1971)
39   C.E. Last, *CW2,* **44** (1945) 142-5
40   J.B. Bailey, *CW2,* **23** (1923) 142
41   R.L. Bellhouse, *CW2,* **55** (1956) 30-45
42   W. Dickinson, *CW1,* 3 (1876-7) 342-7
43   R.L. Bellhouse, *CW2,* **56** (1957) 56-61, *CW2,* **71** (1971) 288-9
44   J. Dixon, *CW1,* 3 (1876-7) 338-40
45   M.C. Fair, *CW2,* **29** (1929) 259-64
46   R.L. Bellhouse, *CW2,* **60** (1960) 25-7

Chapter 3

1   For fuller historical accounts of the Dark Ages see:
      R. Millward and A. Robinson, *The Lake District* (1970) 123-50;
      W. Rollinson, *A History of Cumberland and Westmorland* (1978) 28-36;
      W. Rollinson, *A History of Man in the Lake District* (1967) 54-73
2   A.E. Dodd and E.M. Dodd, *Peakland Roads and Trackways* (1980) 45-53
3   *Anglo-Saxon Chronicle*
4   C.M.L. Bouch and G.P. Jones, *The Lake Counties, 1500-1830* (1961) 33
5   W. Rollinson (1967), *op cit,* 78-81
6   F. Grainger and W.G. Collingwood, *Register and Records of Holm Cultram* (Kendal,
      1929) 21-2, 96; J. Brownbill (ed), 'The Coucher Book of Furness Abbey' vol II,
      Chetham Soc NS **76** (1916) 575
7   C.M.L. Bouch, *Prelates and People of the Lake Counties* (1948) 87-8
8   *Westmorland Gazette,* 17 June 1983
9   P.V. Kelly, *CW2,* **27** (1927) 198-204; J. Melville and J.L. Hobbs, *CW2,* **45** (1945) 129-
      33
10   Grainger and Collingwood, *op cit,* 61-6
11   *ibid,* 10, 12, 15, 33
12   W. Farrer, *Records of Kendale* II (1924) 169, 185, 268, 366, 379
13   *ibid,* 343
14   F.W. Ragg, *CW2* 14 (1914) 7, 29
15   F.W. Ragg, *CW2* 9 (1909) 271

16 English Place Name Society, *The Place Names of Westmorland* (Part 1) (1964-5) 21
17 C.M.L. Bouch, *op cit*, 36-7;
   M. Beresford and H.P.R. Finberg, *English Medieval Boroughs* (1973)
18 B.P. Hindle, *Medieval Roads* (1982) 22, 46
19 J.F. Curwen, *Castles and Towers....* (Kendal, 1913)
20 C.T. Flower, 'Public Works in Medieval Law', vol ii, *Seldon Society* **40** (1923) xvi
21 Bouch and Jones, *op cit*, 18
22 B.P. Hindle, 'The Towns and Roads of the Gough Map' *The Manchester Geographer* **1** (1980) 35-49
23 B.P. Hindle, 'Medieval Roads in the Diocese of Carlisle' *CW2* **77** (1977) 83-95

Chapter 4

1 L.T. Smith, *The Itinerary of John Leland* (5 vols) (1906-10) Part 7, 11-12; Part 9, 46-56, 61; Part 11, 146-7
2 W. Harrison, 'Description of Britain' *in Holinshed's Chronicles*, (1586) i, 192
3 *ibid*, i, 416, 418
4 W. Smith, *The Particular Description of England* (1588)
5 J. Ogilby, *Britannia* (1675) (Facsimile; Amsterdam, 1970)
6 R. Morden, *The County Maps from William Camden's Britannia, 1695* (Newton Abbot, 1972)
7 C. Morris (Ed), *The Illustrated Journeys of Celia Fiennes* (1982) 165-72
8 D. Defoe, *A Tour Thro' the Whole Island of Great Britain* (1724-6) ed G.D.H. Cole (1927) 678-88
9 W. Lawson, *CW2* **79** (1979) 109-19
10 T.H. Hodgson, *CW2* **2** (1902) 274-81
11 T.A. Bainbridge, *CW2* **47** (1948) 183-98; *CW2* **52** (1953) 106-13
12 A. Young, *A Six Months Tour through the North of England* (1770) vol IV, 579-80
13 N. Nicholson, *The Lakers – The First Tourists* (1955)
14 P. Toynbee and L. Whibley, *The Correspondence of Thomas Gray* (Oxford, 1935) 1074-1104
15 *ibid*, 1088
16 W. Hutchinson, *An Excursion to the Lakes* (1776)
17 *ibid*, 120, 176, 200, 229, 249
18 *ibid*, 126
19 T. West, *A Guide to the Lakes* (1778)
20 *ibid*, (2nd ed, 1780) vii, 9, 90-1, 94-5, 99, 102, 132, 139, 161, 169, 188-90
21 T. West, *The Antiquities of Furness* (1774; reprinted Beckermet, 1977)
22 Copies of most of the maps mentioned in this section can be found in Local History Libraries and Record Offices.
23 W. Yates, 'A Map of the County of Lancashire, 1786' *Trans Hist Soc Lancs & Ches* (1968). A facsimile of the map is obtainable from the Lancashire Record Office, Preston.
24 P. Crosthwaite, *Accurate Maps of the Principal Lakes* (ed W Rollinson) (1968)
25 Cumbria is covered on sheets 4, 5, 7, 8, 11, 15 and 19.

Chapter 5

1 K.J. Bonser, *The Drovers* (1970)
2 W. Farrer, *Records of Kendale*, II (Kendal, 1924) 417
3 A. Raistrick, *Green Roads in the Mid-Pennines* (1978)
4 J.D. Marshall, *Old Lakeland* (1971), 88, 92
5 W.T. McIntire, *CW2* **39** (1939) 152-70
6 **ibid**, 92-6
7 W. Farrer, *op cit*
8 J.D. Marshall, *op cit*, 86
9 *ibid*, 80-5
10 J. Housman, *A Topographical Description of Cumberland, Westmorland and Lancashire* (1800) 44, 182-4
11 J.F. Curwen, *Records of Kendale*, III (1926) 150-1

12   J.D. Marshall, *op cit*, 83-5
13   J.F. Curwen, *op cit*, 151
14   C. Morris, *The Illustrated Journeys of Celia Fiennes* (1982) 166
15   M.C. Fair, *CW2* **22** (1922) 98-100
16   W.G. Collingwood, *CW2* **28** (1928) 120-8
      F.W. Cotton 'Packhorse Bridges of the Lake Counties', *Proc Barrow Naturalists' Field Club*, 9 (1963) 23-7
17   J.C. Barringer, *Lakeland Landscape* (1970) 100
18   J.F. Curwen, *The Later Records relating to North Westmorland* (Kendal, 1932) 9
19   R. Orrell, *Saddle Tramp in the Lake District* (1979)
20   *ibid*, 102
21   J.B. Barber and G. Atkinson, *Lakeland Passes* (1927)
      W.T. Palmer, *Byways in Lakeland* (1952) 99-113
22   Barber and Atkinson, *op cit*, 57
      M. Lefebure, *Cumberland Heritage* (1970) 38-46
23   A. Wainwright, *The Southern Fells* (1960) Great End 7
24   *ibid*, Rossett Pike 3-4
25   A. Wainwright, *The Outlying Fells of Lakeland* (1974) 114-19
26   Baddeley's *English Lake District* (1913) 148-9
      Ward Lock's *English Lake District* (1917-18) 121
27   A. Wainwright, *The Western Fells* (1966) Great Gable 7-8; personal communication from Molly Lefebure, April 1984.
28   J.L. Hobbs, *CW2* **55** (1956) 287-91
29   W.G. Collingwood, *Elizabethan Keswick* (Kendal 1912)
      F.J. Monkhouse, *Geography* **28** (1943) 107-13
30   W.G. Collingwood, *op cit*, 28-9
31   J.D. Marshall and M. Davies-Shiel, *Industrial Archaeology of the Lake Counties* (1977) 100-1
32   T. Pape, *The Sands of Morecambe Bay* (Morecambe, 1947) 23
33   *ibid*, 42
34   J. Fell, *CW1* **7** (1884) 1-26
35   T. Pape, *op cit*, 17-19
36   *Cumberland Pacquet*, 11 September 1781
37   T.H. Bainbridge, *CW2* **47** (1948) 185
38   T. West, *A Guide to the Lakes* (1780) 25-6, 28-9
39   J. Lofthouse, *The Curious Traveller: Lancaster to Lakeland* (1956) 19-26, 68-71
      C. Robinson, *Sand Pilot of Morecambe Bay* (1980)
40   J. Lofthouse, *op cit*, 70

Chapter 6
1   S. & B. Webb, *The Story of the King's Highway* (1913) 16-21
2   L.A. Williams, *Road Transport in Cumbria in the Nineteenth Century* (1975) 27. This is essential reading, even though he is mainly concerned with the operation and demise of the turnpikes.
3   M.A. Logie, *CW2* **71** (1971) 86-9
4   W. Albert, *The Turnpike Road System in England, 1663-1840* (1972)
      E. Pawson, *Transport and Economy – The Turnpike Roads of Eighteenth Century Britain* (1977)
5   *Commons Journal* (1739) 461
6   13 Geo II c14 (1739) 311, 315
7   23 Geo II c40 (1750)
8   L.A. Williams, *op cit*, 124-6
9   C.M.L. Bouch, *Prelates and People of the Lake Counties* (1948) 179
10   W. Withers, *Ancient Trackway over Shap Fells* (1970) (Kendal RO)
11   J.F. Curwen, *Records of Kendale*, III (Kendal, 1926) 11
12   L.A. Williams (*op cit*). But beware of his map and list of turnpikes.
13   W. Hutchinson, *The History of the County of Cumberland* (1794) Vol II 120-1
14   L.A. Williams, *op cit*, 172-5

15   *ibid*, 118-9
16   J.F. Curwen, *op cit*, 15, 17
      J.F. Curwen, *Later Records of North Westmorland* (Kendal, 1932), 6-8
17   J.L. Hobbs, *CW2* **55** (1956) 250-65. See also 266-86
18   J. Stockdale, *Annals of Cartmel* (1872) 367-9
19   J.A. Barnes, *CW2* 4 (1904) 207-10
20   L.A. Williams, *op cit*, 81
21   J.F. Curwen, *Records of Kendale* III, (1926) 249
      This also has detail of road changes at Levens, Sampool, Milnthorpe and Heversham,
      see 217, 220, 229, 231
22   J. Melville and J.L. Hobbs, *CW2* **46** (1946) 77-107
23   L.A. Williams, *op cit*, 114

Chapter 7
1   M. Turner, *English Parliamentary Enclosure* (1980)
2   W.G. Hoskins, *The Making of the English Landscape* (1955) 200-4;
      C. Taylor, *Roads and Tracks of Britain* (1979) 171-7
3   L.A. Williams, *Road Transport in Cumbria in the Nineteenth Century* (1975) 86-8
4   J. Stockdale, *Annals of Cartmel* (1872) 340; roads listed 370-82
5   *ibid*, 296-7
6   Lancashire Record Office, Preston: DDCa 21/27
7   J.C. Curwen, writing in 1815. See E. Hughes, *North Country Life in the Eighteenth
      Century* II (1965) 379
8   W. Dickinson, *Agriculture of East Cumberland* (1853) 10
9   J. Norden, *Surveior's Dialogue* (1607)
10   B.P. Hindle, *Lakeland Roads*, (1977) 23-5

Index

References to maps or photographs are set in **bold** type.